confinement and flight

An Essay on English Literature
of the Eighteenth Century

"Carcere IX," second state, by Giovanni Battista Piranesi. (Courtesy
Achenbach Foundation for Graphic Arts, Fine Arts Museums of San Francisco.)

confinement
and flight

An Essay on English Literature
of the Eighteenth Century

w. b. carnochan

University of California Press

Berkeley · Los Angeles · London

University of California Press
Berkeley and Los Angeles, California
University of California Press, Ltd.
London, England
Copyright © 1977 by
The Regents of the University of California
ISBN 0-520-03188-1
Library of Congress Catalog Card Number: 75-46034
Printed in the United States of America

For Nancy Carnochan

Contents

Preface ix

I Captive Souls 1

II Islands of Silence 26

III Prisons, Pastorals, and Warders 60

IV "Which Way I Fly . . ." 102

V Johnson in Fetters 147

VI "Like Birds i' th' Cage":
The Poet and the Happy Man 171

Texts Cited 193

Index 197

Preface

THE intellectual origins of this book probably stem from my reading of Michel Foucault's *Madness and Civilization*, especially the chapter called "The Great Confinement"; its psychological origins probably are rooted in a visit, seven or eight years ago, to the caves of Altamira, home of the stone-age hunters and citadel of their high culture. Foucault's book concerns itself with cultural sea-changes associated with the onset of the modern world; the hunters of Altamira painted the miraculous animal figures on the walls and ceilings of their caves several thousand years ago. What we sometimes think of as the thrilling discoveries of modernity are as likely as not to have had a permanent life in the human mind. That is the case, decidedly, with confinements and flights.

I am going to be taking for granted, however, what Roger Sale (in *Modern Heroism*) has called "the Myth of Lost Unity"; I believe the caves at Altamira offer some empirical evidence that it has a basis in historical fact. The cave paintings represent a great act of reconciliation—mind gathering in the stuff of experience, then making windows in the cave of consciousness and giving a final, precise shape to the fluctuations of subject and object. Surely we have lost something of value in the years that have fallen between the caves and ourselves. But seriously to test the myth of lost unity would be another project than the one at hand.

A history of the modern would also be something different from this. Although I claim the English eighteenth century for modernity, I do so without attending much to discriminations that would be important in any history: How do ironic modes in writers like Swift and Pope differ from those of Romanticism or those of the twentieth century? Is the dialectic of Romanticism a rhetorical sleight-of-hand or a qualitative shift of value? And when did God die anyway?—it seems as if He has had at least nine lives. These are the kinds of questions that would be central, were this a different sort of enterprise.

To specify what kind of an enterprise this is raises the specter of what is barbarously called "methodology." I prefer to call it "method" and mostly to let it speak for itself. But I believe it to be more conservative—indeed conventional—than might at first appear. There is nothing startling about first setting the terms of the argument, identifying some prefatory and exemplary instances in Piranesi, Berkeley, Pascal, and Rochester, and then going on to a closer inspection of specific texts. Despite the occasional interpretative flyer, to see how far the argument might be made to go, I aim to say something textually precise about *Robinson Crusoe, Tristram Shandy, Coopers Hill, The Vanity of Human Wishes,* and so on—not merely to see in them the reverberant themes of confinement and flight.

Beginning with the likes of Piranesi and Pascal, however, one risks excessive solemnity, fear, trembling, and oracular utterance. When modernity does not retreat into silence, it cultivates the oracular style that goes with contemplations of all or nothing. Beginning with Pascal, therefore, one is in danger of underplaying the sportive side of the century that followed Pascal's—and that is always a mistake. As a specific, before beginning, I offer this amiable piece of eighteenth-century verse:

> E'ery Island's but a Prison,
> Strongly bounded by the Sea.
> Kings and Princes for that Reason,
> Pris'ners are, as well as we.
>   Ned Ward [?], *The Prisoner's Opera* (1730)

In the making of this book, many people have helped with useful criticism, timely information, attention to detail, careful typing, editorial exactitude. They include, in alphabetical order, William Allan, John Bender, Bertrand Bronson, Mary Butler, Max Byrd, Martha Campbell, Michael Channing, Joaquim Coelho, Donald Davie, David Donaldson, Lorenz Eitner, Robert C. Elliott, Brigitte Fields, Josephine Guttadauro, Janice Haney, Herbert Lindenberger, John Loftis, Catherine Parke, Helen Pellegrin, Branwen Pratt, Claude Rawson, David Riggs, Lucio Ruotolo, Anne Scowcroft, Richard Scowcroft, Stephen Steinberg, Wilfred Stone, and Ian Watt. To Herbert Lindenberger and Richard Scowcroft I owe the special obligation due those who have first taken into their ken, generously and protectively, the sheltered product of one's thought. To William McClung and others at the University of California Press, I express thanks for their enthusiasm, tolerance for an author's whims, and wise restraint. I am grateful to the School of Humanities and Sciences, Stanford University, for a summer grant that helped me finish the book. Finally, my thanks to Betsy Jablow for doing the index.

I

Captive Souls

But Fate forbids: the Stygian floods oppose
And with nine circling streams the captive souls enclose.
Virgil, Aeneid, VI: 594–595 (*trans. Dryden*)

On the first page of *Miracle of the Rose*, Genet celebrates the prison as the origin of love: "If the rigors of life make us seek out a friendly presence, I think it is the rigors of prison that drive us toward each other in bursts of love without which we could not live; unhappiness is the enchanted potion."[1] This gathers up much that is characteristic of the prison and its literature: its Gothic sense of magical presences ("enchanted potion"), its unnatural rigors and psychological violence, its dialectic of stasis and spasmodic movement, its frustration of normal sexuality as well as its compensatory releases. But it does more, too. By redeeming what has become ordinary, Genet aims to recover the sac-

[1] Trans. Bernard Frechtman (New York: Grove Press, 1966), p. 1.

1

ramental, whether in the vision of the prison as sanctuary or as a lost world of pastoral childishness. Mystic and metaphysician, he retrieves the sacred meanings of prison life from the wreck of history.

The wreckage is the wreckage of the ordinary. Our literature echoes with the sound of chains, breaking the larger silences of the dungeon. Victor Brombert sums up: "Oneiric moods, the descent into a private hell, immurement within the confines of the mind, the oppression of madness, the experience of Time and Nothingness, have habitually found their expression through the basic prison metaphor."[2] We discern the shape of our experience in the shape of prison life. The metaphor, its variants, and the corollary metaphors of escape or flight are so common there's scarcely an undergraduate who can't discourse deeply about the prison house of self. One example will serve for the time being: the first words spoken by the narrator of Joseph Heller's *Something Happened* are "I get the willies when I see closed doors."[3]

Associating these metaphors of confinement and flight with "the weary genius of modernism,"[4] we typically construe the modern to mean since 1780 or thereabouts. My proposition is that writers throughout the English eight-

[2]"Pétrus Borel, Prison Horrors, and the Gothic Tradition," *Novel*, 2 (Winter, 1969): 151–152. See also Brombert's "The Happy Prison: A Recurring Romantic Metaphor," in *Romanticism: Vistas, Instances, Continuities*, ed. David Thorburn and Geoffrey Hartman (Ithaca, N.Y.: Cornell University Press, 1973), pp. 62–79.

[3](New York: Knopf, 1974), p. 3.

[4]Paul Zweig, *The Adventurer* (New York: Basic Books, 1974), p. 171. Zweig's chapter on *Robinson Crusoe* and his chapter on Gothic fiction, called "The Great Escape," take up some of the same themes that I do here. His thesis that "the adventure of escape belongs to the nineteenth century" (p. 171) perpetuates a distinction, I think mistaken in emphasis, between the experience of the eighteenth and nineteenth centuries.

eenth century knew in their bones, if not always in their minds, that they lived in a new world; and that this knowledge decisively affected their handling of metaphors that were to be staples of Romantic and modern literature. I believe it is a modest proposition; history does not always oblige us with Hegelian tidiness, and we need not discover anticipations of ourselves in every nook and cranny.

But if the artists of the eighteenth century were not responsive to the new world rather than just retreating from it, they were unlike any other artists in history. True, many people, including Jonathan Swift and Samuel Johnson, subscribed to the Thirty-Nine Articles of the Church of England. But how likely is it that the art of such writers as Swift and Johnson did not share in the rhythms of change? As it becomes harder to keep up with the gathering speed and specialization of knowledge, we fall more and more under the influence of atmospheric forces whose effects we can roughly understand even when we have only an approximate sense of the forces themselves. How well, after all, do most of us really understand Freud? How well do we understand Heisenberg's uncertainty principle? And yet, no matter how skimpy or approximate our knowledge, who would deny the influence of Freud or Heisenberg? And it is artists, being especially sensitive to atmospheric forces, who are best able to render them as experience as well as to intuit their predictive value for the future.

When Brombert speaks of the "basic prison metaphor," he points up an intriguing fact. Prisons are real, but we characteristically think of them as standing metaphors of existence: to talk of the "basic prison metaphor" is to show how smoothly, here, reality slips over into the service of representation—and how, by the same token, we think of mental states as real confinements. The line that separates the real from the metaphorical thing is in this case very thin and easily crossed. It could be argued, even, that reality follows rather than precedes metaphor, that the history of real prisons recapitulates the history of the philosophical prisons that haunted the eighteenth-century imagination. Granted that institutions of confinement served a special purpose in a world that required new sources of labor, still it is not until the nineteenth century that the prison reform movement succeeded in reducing prison life to the condition of solitariness and silence that Pascal regarded as the human condition. The silent oakum-pickers at the Middlesex House of Correction and the inmates at worship in Pentonville (see accompanying illustrations) are chilling tributes to Victorian efficiency and the gospel of work. They are still more chilling emblems of lives shut off from other lives in permanent, silent solitude.[5] It is as if the reformers,

[5]The engravings reproduced are two among many, taken from photographs, in Henry Mayhew and John Binny, *The Criminal Prisons of London and Scenes of Prison Life* (London: Charles Griffin, 1862). Mayhew's description (pp. 135–136) of a "refractory cell" at Pentonville will convey the power of this extraordinary sequel to his *London Labour and the London Poor*:

"Would you like to step inside," asked the warder, "and see how dark it is when the door is closed?"

We entered the terrible place with a shudder, for there is something intensely horrible in absolute darkness to all minds, confess it or not as they may; and as the warder shut the door upon us—and we felt the cell walls shake and moan again, like a tomb, as he did so—the utter darkness was, as Milton sublimely says—"*visible*." The eyes not only saw, but *felt* the absolute negation of their sense in such a place. Let them strain their utmost, not one luminous chink or crack could the sight detect. Indeed, the very air seemed as impervious to vision as so much black marble, and the body seemed to be positively encompassed with the blackness, as if it were buried alive, deep down in the earth itself. Though we remained several minutes in the hope that we should shortly gain the use of our eyes, and begin to make out, in the thick dusk, bit after bit of the apartment, the darkness was at the end of the time quite as impenetrable as at first, so that the continual straining of the eyeballs, and taxing of the brains, in order to get them to do their wonted duty, soon produced a sense of mental fatigue, that we could readily understand would end in conjuring up all kinds of terrible apparitions to the mind.

"Have you had enough, sir?" inquired the warder to us, as he re-opened the door, and whisked the light of his lantern in our eyes.

"Large oakum-room (under the silent system) at the Middlesex House of Correction, Coldbath Fields."

(Henry Mayhew and John Binny, *The Criminal Prisons of London*, London: Charles Griffin, 1862.)

"The chapel, on the 'separate system,' in Pentonville Prison, during divine service." (Henry Mayhew and John Binney, *The Criminal Prisons of London*, London: Charles Griffin, 1862.)

though justifying their program on grounds of piety and social utility, had in their heads a covert belief that we lodge in Pascal's "petit cachot," a little cell lost in some small corner of an infinite universe. It is as if oakum-picking, absurd occupation that it is, were another of the labors of Tantalus.

What this study will mostly deal with, therefore, is confinement in its extended sense, which can be broken down into epistemological and metaphysical aspects. That division, though it puts asunder what is in nature intimately joined, has the virtue of making it possible to specify an emphasis, and the emphasis of this study falls more on metaphysical than epistemological prisons—more, that is, on the state of being that generates our epistemological crisis than on the crisis itself.

Like the real prisons of the nineteenth century, epistemological prisons derive their character from what is felt as a larger set of conditions; they are, so to speak, an abstracted image of the desire to break out and to make contact with the world beyond the self. Therefore they are felt as almost wholly pernicious. Who suffers willingly the deprivation that follows from the Lockean version of mind as screened off from reality and the external world, receiving only shadowy projections of things as they are? It is one thing to be cut off from other people; some believe that good fences do make good neighbors. It is another thing to be cut off from the fulfillment of questions answered and curiosities appeased. Who does not have the *cacoethes sciendi*, the crude itch to know? Keats credited Shakespeare with the rare virtue of negative capability, the capacity to live without restless grasping for the factual. But there has been only the one Shakespeare.

When we come to the metaphysical prisons from which their epistemological counterparts derive, what we discover is not singlemindedness but a resonant doubleness of feeling. We can track this to its source in the episode that more decisively than any other ushered in the modern world: the demolition of the closed world and its replacement by the infinite universe.[6] The seventeenth-century intuition of infinitude and the invigoration of its paradoxes brought to a pitch the double feelings of wanting to soar and not wanting to, of hating confinement and cherishing it, of being fixed in place and being lost in a great nowhere with nothing to hang on to. That is to say, it rendered in its fullness an experience that epistemological prisons render only half of. It was adjusted to man's nature as "half-open being."[7] The record of eighteenth-century thought is one of strategies and adjustments brought on by this new recognition of our nature. Almost all the strategies on view in this book have one thing in common: they are not strategies of denial. There are no great chains of being here. There is instead a persistent, if not quite universal, recognition of doubleness: "La hantise de l'espace et la hantise de la privation d'espace,"[8] the obsession with space and the obsession with confinement. Though we recognize these feelings

[6]Alexandre Koyré, *From the Closed World to the Infinite Universe* (Baltimore: Johns Hopkins Press, 1957), charts the intellectual course by which the infinite universe came into being.

[7]Gaston Bachelard, *The Poetics of Space*, trans. Maria Jolas (Boston: Beacon Press, 1969), p. 222.

[8]Georges Poulet, "Piranèse et les poètes romantiques français," in *Trois Essais de mythologie romantique* (Paris: Librairie José Corti, 1966), p. 156.

in De Quincey and Vigny and Hugo and Baudelaire, we have yet to notice them in a writer like Defoe.[9]

"La hantise de l'espace et la hantise de la privation d'espace" is Georges Poulet on Piranesi. Nothing could gather up more decisively our mixed responses to infinitude than the *Carceri*, Piranesi's imaginary prisons; and of all that vertiginous series, none is more forthright about the dialectical interchanges between limit and limitlessness than Plate IX, the frontispiece to this book. On the one hand, there is the familiar labyrinth of unfinished spheres and circles, stairways to nowhere, vanishing perspectives, all against a background of clouds and sky that seems variously to be framed by or infinitely far removed from the architectural fantasy of spheres, circles, and stairways. On the other hand, a doorway of massive stone on which the dominant spherical shape in the top half of the engraving seems at first to rest. But isn't it a *trompe l'oeil?* On a second look, the sphere seems to rest on another circular shape or part of another sphere, which seems in turn to intersect with still another (except that this one is part archway) somewhere behind, or even within, the stone cell. In fact, perhaps the cell is no cell at all, but only a façade. The effect of this interplay is both to frighten and to beckon with threats of ecstasy and hopes of incarceration. But all things considered, we can hardly help hoping that the cell is not an illusion, that it does offer the comfort of determinate loca-

[9]See Poulet, *ibid.;* Luzius Keller, *Piranèse et les romantiques français: le mythe des escaliers en spirale* (Paris: Librairie José Corti, 1966); Catharine Savage, " 'Cette Prison Nommée la Vie': Vigny's Prison Metaphor," *Studies in Romanticism,* 9 (1970): 99–113; and, for De Quincey, J. Hillis Miller, *The Disappearance of God: Five Nineteenth-Century Writers* (Cambridge, Mass.: Harvard University Press, 1963), pp. 17–80.

tion. The fear Kepler had expressed, early in the seventeenth century, at the prospect of an infinite universe—
"This very cogitation carries with it I don't know what secret, hidden horror; indeed one finds oneself wandering
in this immensity, to which are denied limits and center
and therefore also all determinate places"[10]—lies at the
heart of many a Gothic wandering and, in the presence
of the *Carceri*, spurs our instinct to find something solid or
some kind of shelter.

Two quite famous philosophical rhapsodies of the age
illustrate these dialectical interchanges, the one in a mood of
elation, the other in a darker mood. The first is in Berkeley's
Dialogues; the second, Pascal's expedition into the empyrean
that comes back down to earth (such flights cannot help
coming back down) with the image of man in his little cell in
a corner of the universe. Different as they are in feeling,
both share the secret hope of domesticating infinitude at the
same time as they wheel and spin and dazzle out in the
reaches of space.

"Look! are not the fields covered with a delightful ver-
dure? Is there not something in the woods and groves, in the
rivers and clear springs that soothes, that delights, that
transports the soul?" Thus Berkeley's Philonous defends
himself against Hylas' charge of skepticism. It is a skillful
bit of rhetoric, preparing the way for the grander excursion
now to come. In the appeal to "something," the *je ne sais quoi*
of the aestheticians, Philonous creates an open-endedness

---

[10]Johannes Kepler, *De stella nova in pede Serpentarii*, chap. 21, quoted in
Koyré, *From the Closed World to the Infinite Universe*, p. 61. The original Latin
is: *Quae sola cogitatio nescio quid horroris occulti prae se fert; dum errare sese quis
deprehendit in hoc immenso, cujus termini, cujus medium ideoque et certa loca
negantur* (*Opera Omnia*, ed. C. Frisch, 8 vols. [Frankfurt and Erlangen:
Heyder & Zimmer, 1858–1871], II: 688). Cf. Miller on these psychological
effects in De Quincey, *The Disappearance of God*, esp. pp. 65–72.

that coexists uneasily with, even if it does not belie, the cool enumeration of pastoral delights. What Berkeley is after is at once to soothe and to transport.[11] It is a neat trick, and he pulls it off with spectacular success as Philonous goes on to contemplate the celestial wonders of creation and, finally, those "immense orbs of light . . . far sunk in the abyss of space."

Now you must call imagination to your aid. The feeble narrow sense cannot descry innumerable worlds revolving round the central fires; and in those worlds the energy of an all-perfect mind displayed in endless forms. But neither sense nor imagination are big enough to comprehend the boundless extent with all its glittering furniture.[12]

In a pedagogical trick that I rather like, I read this passage, all but the last of it, and then put a question: "How do you expect this sentence to end: 'But neither sense nor imagination are big enough to comprehend the boundless extent with all its glittering_____'?" The guesses, ranging from the ordinary ("lights") to the more inventive ("panoply"), put Berkeley's *tour de force* into sharper relief. Though "furniture" is by now a word of diminished value, no exegesis of its eighteenth-century meanings effaces the surprise of discovering that it is the word Berkeley actually used. Nor should it. Then, as now, furniture was what furnished houses: Johnson's first definition is "moveables;

[11]Cf. A. D. Nuttall, *A Common Sky: Philosophy and the Literary Imagination* (Berkeley and Los Angeles: University of California Press, 1974), pp. 35ff. Nuttall's book contains a critique of the prison metaphor as a convention of modern epistemology and literature. I make a different judgment on Berkeley's rhapsody, and stress parts of it that Nuttall does not, but I think our readings are compatible.

[12]*Three Dialogues between Hylas and Philonous*, in Vol. II of *The Works of George Berkeley, Bishop of Cloyne*, ed. A. A. Luce and T. E. Jessop (London: Thomas Nelson & Sons, 1948–1957), pp. 210–211.

goods put in a house for use or ornament." Berkeley has domesticated the void as decisively as the ancients who, peering into the heavens, discovered such domestic items as the belt of Orion and Cassiopeia's chair. Where Pascal returns to a little cell, Berkeley creates a well-appointed and well-lit room of his own. After so conclusive a triumph, no wonder he turns rhapsode: "Is not the whole system immense, beautiful, glorious beyond expression and beyond thought!"[13] The answer is No, not beyond thought nor beyond imagination, since it is Berkeley's imagination that has created some creature comforts in the abyss of space.

No matter how different in spirit, Berkeley and Pascal both need to take cover. To understand the full force of Pascal's flight of the imagination, the feelings that go with it, and especially the feelings that accompany his coming back down to earth, the only thing to do is to hear him out. Since infinitude beggars description, its effects demand recreation. That is what Pascal aims for:

Que l'homme contemple donc la nature entière dans sa haute et pleine majesté, qu'il éloigne sa vue des objets bas qui l'environnent. Qu'il regarde cette éclatante lumière, mise comme une lampe éternelle pour éclairer l'univers que la terre lui paraisse comme un point au prix du vaste tour que cet astre décrit et qu'il s'étonne de ce que ce vaste tour lui-même n'est qu'une pointe très délicate à l'égard de celui que les astres qui roulent dans le firmament embrassent. Mais si notre vue s'arrête là, que l'imagination passe outre; elle se lassera plutôt de concevoir, que la nature de fournir. Tout ce monde visible n'est qu'un trait imperceptible dans l'ample sein de la nature. Nulle idée n'en approche. Nous avons beau enfler nos conceptions, au-delà des espaces imaginables, nous n'enfantons que des atomes, au prix de la réalité des choses. C'est une sphère infinie dont le centre est partout, la circonférence nulle part. Enfin c'est le plus grand caractère sensible de la toute-puissance de Dieu que notre imagination se perde dans cette pensée.

Que l'homme, étant revenu à soi, considère ce qu'il est au prix

[13]*Ibid.*, p. 211.

de ce qui est, qu'il se regarde comme égaré dans ce canton dé-
tourné de la nature; et que de ce petit cachot où il se trouve logé,
j'entends l'univers, il apprenne à estimer la terre, les royaumes, les
villes et soi-même son juste prix. Qu'est-ce qu'un homme dans
l'infini?[14]

Anaphora approximates, rhetorically, an infinite series,
and the anaphoric catalogue stretches on and on: let man
contemplate, let him gaze, let him marvel. And, when he
has reached the limits of vision, let his imagination roam
"beyond." Even there, beyond, nature will furnish more
than mind can conceive of. There is little of comfort, only
grandeur, in this celestial furniture. But for all Pascal's wish
to humble man before God and the infinite, we feel exu-
berance as his rhetoric swoops and soars. Leaving selfhood
behind and losing one's bearings in the infinite is a heady

---

[14]Blaise Pascal, *Pensées*, ed. Léon Brunschvicg, 3 vols. (Paris: Librairie
Hachette, 1904), I: 72-74. ("Let man then contemplate all of nature in its
great and full majesty, let him turn his sight from the low objects that
surround him, let him gaze on that brilliant light set like an eternal lamp to
illuminate the universe, let the earth appear to him as a speck in comparison with the vast circle of the sun, and let him marvel that this vast circle
itself is only a tiny dot compared to the circle of the stars as they roll about
the firmament. But if our view stops there, let imagination pass beyond; it
will sooner grow weary of imagining than nature of providing material for
it to work upon. The whole visible world is no more than an imperceptible
particle in the ample bosom of nature. No idea comes near it. Even if we
enlarge our conceptions beyond all imaginable space, we only bring forth
atoms compared to the reality of things. It is an infinite sphere, of which the
center is everywhere, the circumference nowhere. It is in fact the greatest
sensible evidence of the omnipotence of God that our imagination loses
itself in that thought.

As he returns to himself, let man compare what he is with what exists, let
him realize that he is lost in this remote corner of the universe, and from the
little cell where he finds himself lodged—I mean the universe—let him
judge the true worth of the earth, of kingdoms, of cities, and of himself.
What is a man in the infinite?") For Pascal's influence in England, see John
Barker, *Strange Contrarieties: Pascal in England during the Age of Reason* (Mon-
treal-London: McGill-Queen's University Press, 1975).

business that spirits more secular than Pascal describe as a
kind of drunkenness. Coming back to earth feels like the
morning-after with its aimlessness and its fierce constric-
tions. On the other hand, is nothing to be said for "ce petit
cachot" where we find ourselves lodged? After so grand a
tour of the skies, it's a shocking comedown, but is it abso-
lutely unwelcome? At least it has penitential value. Better
still, it has walls to touch, so we do not utterly lack knowledge of where we are. And if we "lodge" in it, hasn't it some
of the conveniences of home? A monkish accommodation,
no doubt, but like Piranesi's elusive cell and Berkeley's
well-appointed universe, Pascal's "petit cachot," promises
relief from random ecstasies.

Ernest Tuveson puts a tantalizing question that needs an
answer. He wonders why "the great crisis of change from an
anthropocentric and geocentric cosmology produced no
cataclysm" in the eighteenth century?[15] Why, that is, was
there not a corresponding crisis of values and faith such as
might have been predicted in the wake of God's retreat to
the reaches of space? The question depends on the assumption that the age was secure in its values. To the extent
that the assumption looks right, one might answer by
pointing variously to mechanisms of denial or to what we
can think of as the mind's permanent flirtation with the
infinite universe. It's unlikely that even the weight of
Christian and Aristotelian thought ever wholly did away
with it. Surely the conception is as old not just as Archytas
of Tarentum, who gets official credit for it, but as old as that
hypothetical ancient who first had the words to frame the
question: What is beyond whatever is beyond? Surely the

---

[15]"Space, Deity, and the 'Natural Sublime,' " *Modern Language Quarterly*,
12 (1951): 31.

question comes into the mind of any child, no matter whether the official science of the age says the universe is closed or curved or whatever else. We do best, therefore, to think of the new universe as releasing instinctive energies of mind and feeling, even though these energies are at least half directed to acts of confinement and self-confinement.

But another way to look at it is to doubt or to qualify the proposition that there was "no cataclysm." If the *Carceri* do not indicate a cataclysm, they represent at very least the deployment of enormous energies to avert one. If Locke did not understand or admit the radically skeptical consequences of his own epistemology, that is because he wanted to have a new world and yet not to taste its bitterness.[16] If Berkeley could only save the case by seeming to do away with our handhold on reality, that is because the case was a desperate one. The age was one of perilous balances, present even in so balanced a writer as Addison.[17] When Addison asks, in his celebratory ode on the "spacious firmament"—

> What though, in solemn Silence, all
> Move round the dark terrestrial ball?
> (lines 17–18)

—the glorious but unreal voice that rejoices in Reason's ear and sings "The Hand that made us is Divine" (line 24) echoes strangely in the stillness.

To this anticipatory calendar of instances, one more should be added. Nothing could be more to the point than

[16]On the skeptical implications of Locke's epistemology, see John Yolton, *John Locke and the Way of Ideas* (Oxford: Oxford University Press, 1956), pp. 72–114.

[17]W. B. C. Watkins, *Perilous Balance: The Tragic Genius of Swift, Johnson and Sterne* (Princeton: Princeton University Press, 1939) is still a valuable commentary.

the case of Rochester, that nostalgia-ridden prophet of the new world. A prophet he definitely was, even if nostalgia finally won out in his spectacular deathbed denial of what he had been. He had acted out his role as cynic and libertine against the paradoxical setting of infinitude. The boundlessness of the world, taken for granted, justified the boundlessness of desire; it also explained why desire, under any guise, was a trap. "Reason," says the speaker of "A Satyr Against Reason and Mankind," is an *ignis fatuus* of the mind, a wandering fire that leads man through swamps and up mountains and then headlong back down into doubt's "boundless" sea. Not so, says the *adversarius*, who like Icarus restored soars up into the empyrean on the wings of rationality:

> Reason, by whose aspiring influence
> We take a flight beyond material sense,
> Dive into mysteries, then soaring pierce
> The flaming limits of the universe,
> Search heaven and hell, find out what's acted there,
> And give the world true grounds of hope and fear.
>
>   (lines 66–71)

Here is the accustomed structure of ascent and return: an imaginary flight "beyond material sense," a diving and soaring in the region "beyond," and then the "true grounds of hope and fear." But all is reduced to smugness, and the poet implies that the flaming limits of the universe—Lucretius' "flammantia moenia mundi"—are themselves *ignes fatui* that allure and delude weary wandering travelers:

> . . . 'tis this very reason I despise:
> This supernatural gift, that makes a mite
> Think he's the image of the infinite,
> Comparing his short life, void of all rest,
> To the eternal and the ever blest;
> This busy, puzzling stirrer-up of doubt
> That frames deep mysteries, then finds 'em out,

> Filling with frantic crowds of thinking fools
> Those reverend bedlams, colleges and schools;
> Borne on whose wings, each heavy sot can pierce
> The limits of the boundless universe;
> So charming ointments make an old witch fly
> And bear a crippled carcass through the sky.
>
> (lines 75–87)

Cutting across the conventional deference to the infinite and the eternal—that is, to the God whose attributes these were —is the subversive paradox that Rochester flourishes like a banner, "the limits of the boundless universe." Divines and philosophers had been looking for a semantic solution to the troubles caused by unbounded space, but Rochester, being neither a divine nor one to trouble himself with semantic problems, turns it all into grotesque sport:

> Borne on whose wings, each heavy sot can pierce
> The limits of the boundless universe;
> So charming ointments make an old witch fly
> And bear a crippled carcass through the sky.
>
> (lines 84–87)

This parody of the dialectic of limit and limitlessness, with its heavy flights, its rough piercing of limits, its unnatural movements, and its atmosphere of perverse sexuality, is Rochester at his best and most prophetic. It is as if he had peered into the future and discovered the immense abyss of Berkeleyan space turning into the scene of obscure rites and strange secret horrors that Kepler never dreamed of, or Pascal's little cell turning into a Gothic torture chamber. It is also as if, in the outcome, Rochester realized he did not like what he had seen. After such a vision and its ironies, his conversion seems fearfully singleminded, a way of setting limits to the boundless universe. It has the flavor of an earlier and, as we're inclined to think, an easier age.

After Rochester, there is no going back to the singlemindedness of deathbed conversions with their hints of *noblesse oblige*. Or not, at least, for the great writers of the new century who were to make their art, almost all of them, out of a persistent double vision. A modern philosopher and exponent of the infinite raises this objection to his own claims: "But what of the fusillade of paradoxes that threaten to undermine [the actual infinite]? Have we any guarantee that the fecundity of the actual infinite is not to be attributed to a latent contradiction? No wonder, then, that the concept should be so fertile: from a contradiction anything what-ever, even the creation of the world, can be logically de-duced, if not *ex nihilo*, then *ex contradictione*."[18] Whatever the answers to these questions, which are beyond the reach of this enquiry, it could be said that eighteenth-century writers, taken all in all, deduced their worlds *ex contradictione*.

These assumptions govern this essay. I have called it an essay to distinguish it from, say, a study—which might seem to promise a more comprehensive survey of the terri-tory, and one that could hardly afford to omit Richardson's *Clarissa*, for example, mentioned here only once or twice and only in passing. Because *Clarissa* is too big a book in every sense to be dealt with summarily and too well put together to be dealt with in bits and pieces, the choice was, so to speak, whether to write only about it or virtually to leave it out. I have left it out. On the other hand, I have not only included but linger over less magisterial texts and individual passages that are crucial: Swift's two city poems, for example; the opening lines of *Coopers Hill*, where Den-ham wrestled with difficult problems intrinsic to the genre he in effect created; *Vathek*. The importance of these and other texts, in the context, will have to speak for itself.

[18]José A. Benardete, *Infinity: An Essay in Metaphysics* (Oxford: Clarendon Press, 1964), p. 270.

In the next chapter, then, I single out three parallel lives: Robinson Crusoe, Gulliver, and Sterne's Uncle Toby—islanders, all of them, lonely figures in an enclosed or self-enclosing landscape. In them the psychology of confinement takes extreme, but not unfamiliar, form. Each has a tropism, enforced or self-sustaining, for silence. They are case histories in the disease of wordlessness.[19] In their stories *things* are substituted, often, for words and feelings. Something has gone wrong sexually: Toby is wounded in the groin, Gulliver has a passion for his horses, Crusoe has no sexual life at all for close to thirty years. Violence threatens or, as in Toby's mock warfare, neutralizes itself in play. It all signifies frustration, and each of these islanders, though with different degrees of awareness, both does and doesn't want to be rescued from himself.

Crusoe and Gulliver and Toby illustrate, to a perfection, the double feelings that make up the psychology of confinement; the literature of the actual prison—or of what Max Byrd has euphoniously called "The Madhouse, the Whorehouse, and the Convent"[20] (and, I would add, the city)—to a greater extent sorts these feelings out. There are happy prisons and unhappy ones, and I go on to some of these. Happy prisons, like those in *Moll Flanders* and *Tom Jones*, lead to release and a kind of resurrection. Unhappy prisons, from which there's no way out but death, enforce wild, spasmodic, and futile motions—like the astonishing and fantastical raptures of Pope's Eloisa. More profound because more complete are fictions that gather up in an ironic synthesis—that is to say, a synthesis more rhetorical

[19]For a critique of the modern cult of silence, see Hayden Carruth, "Fallacies of Silence," *Hudson Review*, 26 (Autumn, 1973): 462–470.

[20]*Partisan Review*, forthcoming.

in the first instance than psychological—the unhappiness and happiness of confinement: that is what Swift's *Tale of a Tub* and John Gay's *Beggar's Opera* do.

But even in more straightforward fictions of the happy or unhappy prison, things are not so simple as they seem, largely because the artist in his own half-articulated, half-detected presence increasingly brings pressure to bear on the work. Where the artist is, nothing is ever simple: being himself subject to time and death, he looks like an arrant tragedian in the midst of any comedy; being able to scratch chaos into some kind of order, he looks like an arrant jester in the face of tragic events. Really, we're apt to think, he *is* impossible, and an egregious instance, worth singling out ahead of time, is H. F., the narrator of Defoe's *Journal of the Plague Year.* Trapped in a city where victims of the plague are dying and being carried away by cartloads, trapped and endlessly watching, he nonetheless makes the best of it by recording what he sees. He resembles no one so much as a Jamesian narrator, unless perhaps it's the warder of Bentham's *Panopticon*, that hopeful liberal project with which, as Aldous Huxley said, Bentham sowed the dragon's teeth.[21] Imagine it: a vast, doughnut-shaped prison, with cells facing inward, and, at the very center, a warden's lodge: "The essence of it consists . . . in the *centrality* of the Inspector's situation, combined with the well known and most effectual contrivances for *seeing without being seen.*" Bentham supposes that the Inspector will be a family man with wife and children, and this is what life in the lodge has to offer them:

It will supply in their instance the place of that great and constant fund of entertainment to the sedentary and vacant in towns, the looking out of the window. The scene, though a confined, would

[21]*Prisons: With the "Carceri" Etchings by G. B. Piranesi* (Los Angeles: Zeitlin & Ver Brugge, 1949), pp. 12–13.

be a very various, and therefore perhaps not altogether an un-amusing one.[22]

One wants to draw back from such entertainment, but it is the sort artists and readers thrive on. Though the plague devastates the city, though the prisoners live solitary lives in their separate cells, still the artist-watcher trapped at the center of it turns the scene into a diversion.[23]

From confinements to flights is a turn of the coin. Jean Starobinski asks, and leaves no doubt about his answer, whether it is only coincidence that the old dream of flight is realized at the end of the eighteenth century.[24] The twin inventions of the balloon and the panorama responded to hopes as various as those of Milton's high-flying Satan or of John Denham in *Coopers Hill* and the other prospect-seeking poets who followed him. The invention of the steam engine responded to hopes as various as those of Tristram Shandy in his flight from death, Caleb Williams in his flight from Falkland, or the Caliph Vathek in his headlong rush to the Halls of Eblis. Everyone wanted to go higher and faster. But, higher or faster, these flights double back on themselves: in them, the farther you fly, the nearer you come to home; there are no limits, no center, no determinate places, and coming home is coming back to an unaltered self. In a sad and self-defeating imitation, these flights reenact the my-

[22]*Panopticon; or, the Inspection-House* (Dublin and London: T. Payne, 1791), pp. 23, 26–27.

[23]I did not see Michel Foucault's new study, *Surveiller et punir: Naissance de la prison* (Paris: Gallimard, 1975), until this book was in press. Foucault points out that if leprosy gave rise to rituals of exclusion, the plague gave rise to programs of discipline; and that our way of dealing with the abnormal amounts to a combining of these procedures: "Le *Panopticon* de Bentham est la figure architecturale de cette composition" (p. 201).

[24]*The Invention of Liberty, 1700–1789*, trans. Bernard C. Swift (Geneva: Skira, 1964), p. 209.

thology of quest. I bring the story in a selective way up as far as Coleridge, Wordsworth, and Keats and their efforts to recover a sense of purposeful movement. I do not bring it up as far as Huck Finn, who lit out for the territory, or to the world of easy riders and midnight cowboys, or to the Golden Gate where so many a flight has come to its Icarian end.

Against these motions of the modern mind, which were characteristic motions of his own mind as well, Samuel Johnson (who comes next) set himself in sturdy, but realistic, opposition. In this setting he looks even more than usual like a tough-minded maverick, indeed even more than usual like a hero. If the manacles and padlock that he committed to the care of Mrs. Thrale were an anticipatory provision for the loss of sanity he feared, or even if they were in some way we cannot know the apparatus of masochism, they also dramatize the less specific restraints of life and language that he everywhere imposed upon himself.[25] Under the guise of observation, his prospect from China to Peru embodies some of his longings, and one point of *The Vanity of Human Wishes* is the deposing of observation—that is to say, of the poet who has summoned up a more than mortal prospect—in favor of a God who alone has a prospect of mankind. Johnson's astronomer and his winged man in *Rasselas*, not to mention his own energetic excursion to the Hebrides, these measure the strength of the appeal that heights and flights and outer limits held for him. When he draws back, refusing (for example) to expatiate in boundless futurity, he draws back from everything that solicited him powerfully. He sums up the claims of a control deriving from what he perceived as necessity. His achievement was to carve out a working relationship with the new world in

[25]See John Wain, *Samuel Johnson* (New York: Viking Press, 1975), pp. 286–292.

the midst of distractions and discords, both private and public.

But Johnson was the rarest of men—and in any case the inner forces that he resisted, striving to put them constructively to work, were more powerful than even he, with his prodigiously quick apprehension of realities, could have guessed. As a summary and recapitulation, I examine another *topos* of the old world, that of the happy man, irresistibly yielding to one of the new, that of the captive artist. The evidence here consists of three poems, two of them famous and the other well-known in its own day: Pope's "Ode on Solitude," John Norris' "My Estate," and William Blake's "How Sweet I Roam'd." So that the final destination will be in sight, here is Blake's poem:

> How sweet I roam'd from field to field,
>   And tasted all the summer's pride,
> 'Till I the prince of love beheld,
>   Who in the sunny beams did glide!
>
> He shew'd me lilies for my hair,
>   And blushing roses for my brow;
> He led me through his gardens fair,
>   Where all his golden pleasures grow.
>
> With sweet May dews my wings were wet,
>   And Phoebus fir'd my vocal rage;
> He caught me in his silken net,
>   And shut me in his golden cage.
>
> He loves to sit and hear me sing,
>   Then, laughing, sports and plays with me;
> Then stretches out my golden wing,
>   And mocks my loss of liberty.

In God's service used to be perfect freedom, but no

longer, especially not when the god is Phoebus Apollo. If, in the imagination of the writers called Augustan, there is a continuous interplay of limit and limitlessness and an awareness of how eternal space had inherited the ontological attributes of divinity,[26] what Blake will eventually try to do is re-invent divinity and thus liberate man from the bonds of paradox. This project, so dear to one corner of the modern mind, is to bound the universe once more by attributing to our own compound of body and imagination the limitlessness of God, thereby giving limits once again while seeming to deny them, giving comfort where comfort is hard to find. In this early poem Blake charts the feelings of entrapment that he later struggled to overcome.

It is not controversial—as perhaps it is in the case of the Augustan writers—to claim Blake for modernity. It is not surprising, therefore, to discover in "How Sweet I Roam'd" a feeling close to that of so modern a *cri de coeur* as this:

But what does it all matter! Captive, captive, I am locked up—can not stir, may do nothing—and outside it is spring, the dark, moist earth is fragrant, the sap is rising, the first flowers are blooming! I would like to hike, to walk to the bright flowered fields of grass and under blossoming bushes listen to the singing of small, loving birds with shining eyes, like set jewels or drops of colored enamel.[27]

Granted that Blake's lyric has its underlying fears and fantasies under better control. But then again this is an actual gleaning from an artist's prison journal: that of Egon Schiele, who went to prison in 1912, having scandalized the

[26]"The infinite Universe . . . inherited all the ontological attributes of Divinity. Yet only those—all the others the departed God took away with Him" (Koyré, *From the Closed World to the Infinite Universe*, p. 276).

[27]Alessandra Comini, *Schiele in Prison* (Greenwich, Conn.: New York Graphic Society, 1973), p. 49.

little village where he lived by his "immorality." It is the way the world outside the prison appears to Schiele's frantic imagination that enforces our sense of likeness to Blake. The blossoming bushes and birds with jewel-like or enameled eyes, like Blake's golden pleasures, are the ornaments of Renaissance pastoral or the figures of Byzantine mosaic. They decorate a lost world.

II

Islands of Silence

ONE WAY to plot the curve of the modern would be to begin with Donne's "No man is an island entire of itself"; and end with, say, Arnold's "Yes! in the sea of life enisled," or with the song from the 1960s, "I am a rock, I am an island." We figure our lives under the metaphor of insularity as readily as that of the prison. We dream of a common continent that has been lost—and sometimes, in daylight hours, set out to find it. The "jungle of vegetation" that gave metaphoric substance to the concept of organic form was one re-creation of the lost territory. So were the visionary worlds of the primitive painters: the jungle of Douanier Rousseau or, in America, Erastus Salisbury Field's lavish Garden of Eden. So, for that matter, was the Africa of Conrad's *Heart of Darkness*—a lost continent but full of terrors. But for every traveler who heads for the interior, two or three more head for the Hebrides, bent on acting out the conditions of island life. That's because we like islands or even love them, like the hero of Lawrence's short story.[1] It wouldn't do to over-

[1] D. H. Lawrence, "The Man Who Loved Islands," in Vol. III of *The Complete Short Stories* (London: William Heinemann, 1955), pp. 722–746.

estimate the ironic tone of "I am a rock, I am an island" at the expense of its pure wishfulness. Nor would it do to overestimate the obsessional futility of Lawrence's hero at the expense of his transient gratifications.[2]

Two texts that render these antithetical feelings in pure and separate form will throw light on the ambivalent island lives, real or self-inflicted, of Crusoe, Gulliver and Uncle Toby. The one is from Rousseau, the other from Pascal. Both are shopworn from handling, and for good reason: between them they exhaust a range of familiar feelings. For Rousseau, l'Isle de Saint Pierre is his lost Eden; his memories of it are full of lavish *tendresse:*

> De toutes les habitations où j'ai demeuré (et j'en ai eu de charmantes), aucune ne m'a rendu si véritablement heureux et ne m'a laissé de si tendres regrets que l'Isle de St. Pierre au milieu du lac de Bienne. Cette petite Isle qu'on appelle à Neufchatel l'Isle de la Motte, est bien peu connue, même en Suisse. Aucun voyageur, que je sache, n'en fait mention. Cependant elle est très agréable et singuliérement située pour le bonheur d'un homme qui aime à se circonscrire.[3]

The island yielded Rousseau a comfortable way of life—

---

[2]On the island motif, see Bernhard Blume, "Die Insel als Symbol in der Deutschen Literatur," *Monatshefte*, 41 (January, 1949): 239–247; and Herbert Lindenberger, "The Idyllic Moment: On Pastoral and Romanticism," *College English*, 34 (December, 1972): 335–351. On theories of organic form, see M. H. Abrams, *The Mirror and the Lamp: Romantic Theory and the Critical Tradition* (New York: Oxford University Press, 1953), pp. 156–225. I have borrowed the phrase "jungle of vegetation" from Abrams, p. 169.

[3]Jean-Jacques Rousseau, *Les Rêveries du promeneur solitaire,* ed. Marcel Raymond, in Vol. I of *Oeuvres complètes,* ed. Bernard Gagnebin and Marcel Raymond (Paris: Gallimard, 1959–1969), p. 1040. ("Of all the places I have lived—and some of them have been charming—none has made me so truly happy and left me with such tender regrets as the island of St. Pierre in the middle of the lake of Bienne. This little island, called in Neuchatel the island of 'la Motte,' is little known, even in Switzerland. No traveller that I know of mentions it. But it is very pleasant and especially well situated for the happiness of a man who loves to circumscribe himself.")

domestic, miniaturized, secure. Its perfection being that of
the past, remoteness is essential. It is little known—"même
en Suisse"; travelers do not mention it. It is just right for
the man "qui aime à se circonscrire." The reflexive verb
confirms the identity of islander and island. To be sure,
Rousseau is committing a kind of treason against himself by
publishing the whereabouts of this little-known island; betrayals and inconsistencies like this constitute the normal
paradoxes of island life. But one need not dwell on the
lurking betrayal, given the resonant evocation of island
languor and self-esteem.

Rousseau's island rests in the middle of a lake, and not a
very big lake at that. The delight of it, we're made to feel,
has to do with its situation at the center of things. The
islander's self-satisfaction stems from being in a position to
see, in a sense to control, the encircling motions of the
world. It is as if Rousseau, "qui aime à se circonscrire," were
responding to Pascal, whose image of life as the condition of
a man waking up on a desert island is more terrifying than
his image of life as bound to a prison cell:

> En voyant l'aveuglement et la misère de l'homme, en regardant
> tout l'univers muet, et l'homme sans lumière, abandonné à lui-
> même, et comme égaré dans ce recoin de l'univers, sans savoir qui
> l'y a mis, ce qu'il y est venu faire, ce qu'il deviendra en mourant,
> incapable de toute connaissance, j'entre en effroi comme un
> homme qu'on aurait porté endormi dans une île déserte et effroy-
> able, et qui s'éveillerait sans connaître [où il est], et sans moyen
> d'en sortir. Et sur cela j'admire comment on n'entre point en
> désespoir d'un si misérable état. Je vois d'autres personnes auprès
> de moi, d'une semblable nature: je leur demande s'ils sont mieux
> instruits que moi; ils me disent que non. Et sur cela, ces misérables
> égarés, ayant regardé autour d'eux, et ayant vu quelques objets
> plaisants, s'y sont donnés et s'y sont attachés.[4]

[4]Blaise Pascal, *Pensées* (see Chap. I, above, note 14), III, 133–134. ("When
I see the blindness and misery of man, when I look on the whole silent

The interchange between the light of the universe and the darkness of the prison cell has been gathered up in a larger darkness. The universe is silent. Man has no light and is blind: he is doubly impotent, both because of what he is and what the universe is around him. His island is deserted and dreadful ("effroyable"): inner and outer conditions reinforce each other. There is only one thing to do—or at least only one thing that most people find to do: "Ces misérables égarés, ayant regardé autour d'eux, et ayant vu quelques objets plaisants, s'y sont donnés et s'y sont attachés." This compensatory attachment to *things* in the darkness and silence sets the stage for one of the modes of realism. The literature of silence, as we're reminded by Ihab Hassan, "aspires to an impossible concreteness."[5]

A thorough study of the psychopathology of island life would deal with its potentiality for violence and its eccentric sexuality as well as its wordlessness, its concurrent pressure to substitute things for words and emotions, and the mixed feelings that islanders have about their lives. Wordlessness and mixed feelings will be most in view here. Crusoe calls his island "a Scene of silent Life" and recognizes the strangeness of talking about it, ". . . such perhaps as was never heard of in the World before" (63); Gulliver moves to a condition of speechlessness; words put Toby's life in

universe and see man without knowledge, abandoned to himself and lost in this corner of the universe, without knowing who has put him there, what his purpose is, what will become of him at death, I become terrified, like a man carried in his sleep to a dreadful desert island who wakes up not knowing where he is and with no way to escape. And then I wonder that one does not utterly despair in such a miserable state. I see others near me in the same condition; I ask them if they know more than I do; they tell me they do not; and with that these miserable lost souls, having looked about and seen some pleasing objects, have given and bound themselves over to them.")

[5]*The Literature of Silence: Henry Miller and Samuel Beckett* (New York: Knopf, 1967), p. 10.

danger. Crusoe amasses his astonishing store of supplies; Gulliver's last speechlessness matches that of the Laputan sages who substitute things for words; Toby revels in maps and fortifications. And all of them, with varying awareness, are of two minds: on the one hand, they want to be rescued from insularity because, like Pascal, they find it full of terrors; on the other, they do not want to be rescued because, like Rousseau, they lead comfortable lives and resent intrusion. If we go on to look at their lives at closer range, we can't help seeming like Toby's Widow Wadman or Lemuel Gulliver's wife, Mary, or even the cannibals in *Crusoe*, invaders of a mock-paradise, full of a devouring good-heartedness. To be sure, Swift and Sterne and Defoe were there first, an irony that we'll come back to.

Robinson Crusoe, then, is mostly Rousseau's man. He has a genius for repose; and when he sounds the woodnotes of wild despair, we sense a stock response:

September 30, 1659. I poor miserable *Robinson Crusoe*, being shipwreck'd, during a dreadful Storm, in the offing, came on Shore on this dismal unfortunate Island, which I call'd *the Island of Despair*, all the rest of the Ship's Company being drown'd, and my self almost dead.

(70)

The island comes from Spenser or Bunyan: *the Island of Despair*. But even without literary analogues, we could recognize from the facts of Crusoe's own story that this is a *paysage moralisé*. By figuring his island allegorically in his journal he tries to distill its meaning. But the meaning he assigns it jars with the narrative rendering of his experience. In the journal all is miserable, dreadful, dismal, unfortunate. In fact, things are not nearly so bad as that. Crusoe's first reaction after being cast ashore is thankfulness for his deliv-

erance. His second reaction, though despairing to the point
of frenzy, is not the reaction of someone who is "almost
dead." He is in a frenzy because he has no weapon and
nothing "about me but a Knife, a Tobacco-pipe, and a little
Tobacco in a Box" (47). There are grains of comfort here,
but again none in the journal: "I had neither Food, House,
Clothes, Weapon, or Place to fly to . . . ." And comparing the
journal version of his first night on land—"I slept in a Tree
for fear of wild Creatures, but slept soundly tho' it rain'd all
Night" (70)—with the real thing, we can't help believing
that Crusoe paints despair and salvation by the numbers.

For to say he slept soundly understates the case. As night
comes, he finds himself "a thick bushy Tree like a Firr, but
thorny" and there determines to "set all Night, and consider
the next Day what Death I should dye . . . ." With this
charming postponement of the inevitable he wedges himself into his tree, arms himself with a stick for self-defense,
and "having been excessively fatigu'd, I fell fast asleep, and
slept as comfortably as, I believe, few could have done in my
Condition, and found my self the most refresh'd with it, that
I think I ever was on such an Occasion" (47). Not only does
he get a good night's rest among the thorns, but he deprives
his desperate condition, in the telling, of its uniqueness as
well as its terrors. It's no longer his first anguished night on
a desert island but one occasion among others, his sleep
perhaps the soundest ever. We aren't surprised, the next
morning, to find him talking about "my Appartment in the
Tree" (48), having transformed the thorn tree into a tidy
bed-sitter. He does not mention the rain that, according to
the journal, fell all night. The rain is an afterthought, an or-
thodox allegory of discomfiture imposed on Crusoe's tal-
ent for being comfortable.

At the same time, his comfort-seeking has an obsessional

side that marks him not only as Rousseau's ally but as one of Pascal's lost ones. If the reading of *Robinson Crusoe* as spiritual biography overlooks experience in favor of its schematizations, so does the reading of it as an economic tract. It is bourgeois psychology on display here—to which spiritual and economic systems are subordinate Crusoe is a collector, one of the greatest ever, an accumulator of "objets plaisants." The psychological function of these objects, much of it, lies concealed behind their utilitarian value. His orgy of removing things from the wrecked ship gathers momentum as the utility of what he takes diminishes until at last, in the case of the gold, it has no value except as it symbolizes pure desire.

Defoe's psychological insight, not the moralizing, is what matters as Crusoe recounts his stripping of the ship. He begins by gathering provisions—"Bread, Rice, three Dutch Cheeses, five Pieces of dry'd Goat's Flesh . . . and a little Remainder of *European* Corn . . ."; a considerable arsenal —"two very good Fowling-pieces," two pistols, powder horns, a bag of shot, "two old rusty Swords," and two barrels of powder; and a store of tools, nails, and the like (50). It all seems sensible and workmanlike, but the enumerative habit of mind—three cheeses, two swords, two barrels of powder—which we may write down as circumstantial realism, should tip us off to the energies that Crusoe's situation has set in motion. What begins as a gathering of useful supplies turns into an acquisitive fury: "I had the biggest Maggazin of all Kinds now that ever were laid up, I believe, for one Man, but I was not satisfy'd still; for while the Ship sat upright in that Posture, I thought I ought to get every Thing out of her that I could; so every Day at low Water I went on Board, and brought away some Thing or other . . ." (55). The sailor's habit of personifying his ship as a woman yields an image so odd that we can hardly help feeling (with Freudian hindsight) that Robinson's collecting instincts derive from his buried sexuality. In any case, things now have a value all out of proportion to their usefulness. It is no longer just a case of Crusoe's getting what he needs, but of getting everything he can, while he can, to add to the biggest store of supplies ever gathered by a single man. The collector is speaking, proud of what he has acquired but restless because no matter how large his store and no matter how far he has outdistanced the competition, he is "not satisfy'd still."

The end of the orgy comes after Crusoe's first fortnight ashore: "I had been now thirteen Days on Shore, and had been eleven Times on Board the Ship; in which Time I had brought away all that one Pair of Hands could well be suppos'd capable to bring, tho' I believe verily, had the calm Weather held, I should have brought away the whole Ship Piece by Piece" (56–57). Like Don Giovanni, with his 640 conquests in Italy, his 231 in Germany, and his rapacious instinct for more, Crusoe displays what the age might have called, had it occurred to anyone to give it a name, the pleasures of enumeration. Robinson Crusoe and Don Giovanni covet everything, but need to have it piece by piece.

Now the wind begins to rise and, sensing a storm, Crusoe decides he had better go over the same ground a second time to be sure he hasn't missed anything. In fact he has, discovering now in a locker drawer "two or three Razors, and one Pair of large Sizzers, with some ten or a Dozen of good Knives and Forks . . . ." How casual-seeming, and how misleading, is the enumeration: two or three razors, ten or a dozen knives. Best to cover up obsession with calculated offhandedness. Crusoe has found a nice reward for the compulsive collector, checker of oversights, and retracer of

footsteps, but more is to come: now he finds the money—
"some *European* Coin, some *Brasil*, some Pieces of Eight,
some Gold, some Silver," to the value of about thirty-six
pounds—that he almost but not quite persuades himself to
let go to the bottom (57). The fact that it's money produces
the stock moralizing that draws attention away from the
progressively stronger hold *things* have gained on him. Did
he really need the dozen or two hatchets or the seven mus-
kets he has taken away already (54)? He has been shoring
up fragments against his own loss. How many of us would
not do what Crusoe does, equipping ourselves with all the
things we could? And who's to say, for that matter, that
Crusoe might not have survived with such a store of pleasing objects to lean on? Bourgeois man, as Henri Lefebvre has
said, is what he has.[6] Crusoe has prepared himself for his
silent life.

Even his playfulness, his mock-futile assertion of mastery
over his island realm, does not alter his dependency; it
merely alters the terms. Like any child emperor, asserting a
compensatory sovereignty over things and circumstances
that have mastered him, he roams his island with an imperial umbrella, patronizes the dog who sits always "at my
Right Hand," and congratulates himself on having not a
rebel among his subjects (148). But feeding into and sup-
porting the fantasy is that enormous store of goods. Without these imperial endowments, sorted, enumerated, and
laid by, Crusoe's lordly manner would produce a kind of
existential farce instead of the witty and plausible mock-
heroic that Defoe actually brings off. Like the combs,
pins, puffs, powders, patches, bibles, and billets-doux
that accompany Belinda's ritual self-worship in *The Rape*

[6] " 'Le bourgeois n'étant que par ce qu'il a . . .' " (quoted in Jean Caze-
neuve, *Bonheur et civilisation* [Paris: Gallimard, 1966], p. 216.)

of the Lock, Crusoe's more utilitarian collection props up an empire.

On the one hand, then, Crusoe luxuriates in his thorn tree and makes the best of it. On the other, he gathers, collects, enumerates, and ultimately depends on the store of things he has put together. The two roles complement each other: it takes a luxuriant imagination to be a collector. So it is not surprising that the comfortable islander Rousseau chooses, as Émile's primer, neither Aristotle nor Pliny nor Buffon but *Robinson Crusoe*. Dependence on men, says Rousseau, is the work of society; dependence on "things," by which he does not mean merely objects but circumstance, the work of nature:

La dépendance des choses n'ayant aucune moralité ne nuit point à la liberté et n'engendre point de vices. La dépendance des hommes étant desordonnée les engendre tous, et c'est par elle que le maitre et l'esclave se dépravent mutuellement.

Remembering that Rousseau wants to knock down the old order of masters and slaves, but then remembering Crusoe's relationship with Friday, we grow uneasy. Like Crusoe, Émile will learn by doing, not by reading, and will amuse himself by masquerading: "Qu'il se voye habillé de peaux, portant un grand bonnet, un grand sabre, tout le grotesque équipage de la figure, au parasol près dont il n'aura pas besoin."[7] This catches not only Crusoe's dependency on

[7]*Émile ou de l'éducation Émile et Sophie*, ed. Charles Wirz and Pierre Burgelin, in Vol. IV of Rousseau, *Oeuvres complètes*, pp. 311, 455. ("Dependence on things, not being a matter of morality, does not put liberty in jeopardy and produces no vices. Dependence on men, being hard to control, produces all the vices, and this is how master and slave corrupt each other." "Let him see himself clothed in skins, wearing a big cap and carrying a big sword, all the grotesque outfit of the role, even the parasol that he won't need.") For the child's dependence on things in Rousseau, see John Charvet, *The Social Problem in the Philosophy of Rousseau* (Cambridge: Cambridge University Press, 1974), pp. 44–45, 65–66.

things and his compensatory effort to rise above them, but the reciprocal relationship between dependency and Crusoe's play: the parasol, "dont il n'aura pas besoin," is the giveaway. Dependency on things asserts itself, even in compensatory play, as a passion for what is surplus and therefore not needed. It is not really play at all.

Impoverished though our myth-making faculties may be, however, we are not reduced to apotheosizing loungers and collectors; and Crusoe is by now a mythical figure.[8] What has done the trick is the episode of the footprint. That episode dominates the book because it dominates (if my experience is a fair test) our memory of it. When he sees the footprint, Crusoe's guard-rails give way: the island ceases to be a comfortable lodging and turns into a region of awe such as Pascal imagined:

Pour moi, je n'ai pu y prendre d'attache, et, considérant combien il y a plus d'apparence qu'il y a autre chose que ce que je vois, j'ai recherché si ce Dieu n'aurait point laissé quelque marque de soi.[9]

Unable to attach himself to the pleasing objects of the world but believing there must be something else besides what he sees, Pascal wonders whether God has not left a sign. In Crusoe's case the sign comes unexpected, unsought, and unwanted, and isn't on any realistic account a sign of divinity; but its emanations and attributes are more than human. That is why the episode of the footprint has in fact the crucial place that memory assigns it.

[8]See Ian Watt, "*Robinson Crusoe* as a Myth," in *Eighteenth-Century English Literature*, ed. J. L. Clifford (New York: Oxford University Press, 1959), pp. 158–179.

[9]Pascal, *Pensées*, III, 134. ("For myself, I have not been able to tie myself to things, and considering how likely it is that there is more than what I see, I have looked about to discover if this God has left no sign of himself.")

It takes place at the dead center of the book and at midday: "It happen'd one Day about Noon going towards my Boat, I was exceedingly surpriz'd with the Print of a Man's naked Foot on the Shore, which was very plain to be seen in the Sand." But we should see how Defoe got to this point. The footprint interrupts a state of island normality, the distillation of Crusoe's genius for regularity and repose. "I used frequently to visit my Boat," he has said in the preceding paragraph, "and I kept all Things about or belonging to her in very good Order." Everything is trim and shipshape. And, since he has had some anxious moments when he has taken the boat too far to sea, now he resolves to stay close to shore: "No more hazardous Voyages would I go, nor scarce ever above a Stone's Cast or two from the Shore, I was so apprehensive of being hurry'd out of my Knowledge again by the Currents, or Winds, or any other Accident." It is the quotidian life of the islander, cheerful about his insularity, a life of things in good order, diversions, and cautious self-regard. Crusoe aims not to be hurried out of his depth any more by currents or winds or accidents. It is the nature of accidents, however, to fall out unexpectedly and beyond our control. "But now," says Crusoe, "I come to a new Scene of my Life" (153).

Nothing else in the book matches the opening of the next paragraph: "It happen'd . . . ." We hover between a reportorial, personal matter-of-factness (we half expect the sentence to go on: "It happened that . . .") and solemn mysteriousness: "It"—whatever it was—"happen'd one Day about Noon going towards my Boat . . . ." As he gathers up the separate island feelings of Rousseau and Pascal, Defoe binds together the fictional worlds of circumstantial realism and of Gothic romance: the realm of technology blends with that of abominable snowmen, big-footed creatures in the

California forest, unidentified flying objects. In that one moment, Defoe apprehends our longing and our dread.

The strangest thing about the footprint is that it is one footprint rather than two or many. What's more, it resists winds and tides: it is still there when Crusoe comes back a few days later. It takes the edge off the experience to ask investigatory questions: What happened to the other footprints, or was there only one in the first place? Why is it impervious to the elements? But the unanswerability of the questions underscores the strangeness. It is not just someone else's presence on his island that affects Crusoe so but the obscurity of a presence that threatens, in ways he can only guess, a life of things in good order and the reciprocal release of self-aggrandizing play: "I stood like one Thunder-struck, or as if I had seen an Apparition." Always on the alert for apparitions, Defoe knows their effects: all Crusoe's senses sharpen at the same time as he draws away from external things. The silence that has become his natural element deepens and changes: "I listen'd, I look'd round me, I could hear nothing, nor see any Thing . . ." (153). This is the paradoxical silence that comes with hearing nothing. And, as if struck blind by the footprint, Crusoe cannot see "any Thing." It is an epiphany, an effacing of the world of ordinary impressions.

"I went up to a rising Ground to look farther," he says, but rising ground and shore merge into one another, no transition between them; "I went up the Shore and down the Shore, but it was all one, I could see no other Impression but that one . . . ." Experience contracts into the single footprint: "I could see no other Impression but that one, I went to it again to see if there were any more, and to observe if it might not be my Fancy; but there was no Room for that" (153–154). Crusoe has no room in his field of vision for anything but the footprint. He is monomaniacal, like Melville's Ahab, who can see nothing in his mind's eye but the white whale. But he has a better set of defenses than Ahab.

Now the synthesis of seeing and experience breaks down: "There was exactly the very Print of a Foot, Toes, Heel, and every Part of a Foot." The world of things is the world of partial experience, and Crusoe returns to analysis, anatomizing the footprint as intensely as he has gathered his store of goods. Mightn't he have been content to know that the footprint had toes and ball and heel? But he insists on more, on "every Part." The pleasures of enumeration are coming back, and Crusoe, though terrified, begins to display some of his old aptitude for the normal: "But after innumerable fluttering Thoughts, like a Man perfectly confus'd and out of my self, I came Home to my Fortification." To be sure, he will have to make strenuous adjustments to recover his self and thus preserve the normal: under this threat of intrusion, his "Home" becomes his "Fortification" and his "Castle" —and "so I think I call'd it ever after this" (154). He does not want to share his island either with man or god. But preserving the normal requires self-deception, for within the limits of his understanding, Crusoe knows what has happened to him. When he puzzles over his inconsistency, wondering why he trembles at the "silent Appearance of a Man's having set his Foot in the Island" when he might have welcomed it, his puzzlement is disingenuous. The forbidding silence of the footstep superimposes itself on the comfortable silence of isolation, and Crusoe shields himself from deeper perceptions of mystery by putting on his best homiletic manners: "To Day we love what to Morrow we hate; to Day we seek what to Morrow we shun; to Day we desire what to Morrow we fear" (156). These curt rhythms and customary moralizings mask the recognition that one silence echoes the other. Which silence we choose depends on whether we look to Pascal or to Rousseau. We know by now where Crusoe's instincts lie.

Even so, he toys with proto-existential fantasies of breaking down the walls. On coming home to his fortification, the first idea that comes into his mind is to tear down his walls, release his cattle, dig up his cornfields, and finally demolish his bower and tent, so that no one will suspect his presence. This fantasy of letting go, even in a spirit of self-protection and fearfulness, implies a release from dependency. But we know Crusoe's not the type, and once more he retreats behind the veils of morality: "O what ridiculous Resolution Men take, when possess'd with Fear!" (159).

Thus morally fortified and self-concealed, he turns to the only alternative for an islander faced with the threat of intruders or the unknown: to barricade himself more and more strongly, as with double bonds. Because the door to his cave opens beyond his protective walls, he resolves to make himself another fortification, using a double row of trees that he has planted—as if with a premonitory instinct—twelve years before. In two years he has a "thick Grove" to strengthen his defenses, and in five or six years an impenetrable, unassailable fortress: "so monstrous thick and strong, that it was indeed perfectly impassable" (161). The only way in and out for the commander of this fortress is by a pair of ladders. All this in the name of "humane Prudence" for the sake of "my own Preservation" (162). If not Crusoe's *own* preservation, whose could it be? The ghostly footstep has made him, like Locke's economic man, possessive of himself; and this self-possessiveness, with its latent pressure toward the contractual, tips the balance of his island life. Though solitary, he has been coextensive with his world. Now he is digging in.

When Crusoe discovers the remains of the cannibal feast, his anxieties push him still further into silence and self-containment. Forgetful of his superior firepower, he no longer dares drive a nail or chop wood or fire a gun or, least of all, make a fire, in case the smoke "which is visible at a great Distance in the Day should betray me." He has become invisible in spite of himself, the instinct that made him think about breaking down all his enclosures having pushed him 180 degrees in the opposite direction. So it is fitting that now, silent, invisible, and less than human, he discovers, "to my unspeakable Consolation," a cave in the earth with a long passage leading to it, so long that no one would venture into it—no one, that is, "but one who like me, wanted nothing so much as a safe Retreat" (176).

A safe and womb-like retreat it does turn out to be, like Gulliver's stables and Uncle Toby's rood and a half of ground. But as if to emphasize the psychological finality of cave-dwelling, Defoe provides Crusoe with second thoughts as he burrows into the earth. Having found "a kind of hollow Place" in the underbrush, he gets "with Difficulty into the Mouth of it" and discovers that the hollow place is a cave large enough to stand up in "and perhaps another with me." The fantasy, touched by the hope that someone might come along to share accommodations in the cave, is almost wistful. But no sooner has Crusoe gone in than he rushes back out, startled by the sight of "two broad shining Eyes of some Creature, whether Devil or Man I knew not, which twinkl'd like two Stars . . . ." The apprehension that perhaps there *is* someone else in the cave, whether man or devil, sheds an ironic light on Crusoe's fantasy that it might have room for two. But he is still of a mixed mind. He seizes a convenient (if incongruous) firebrand, runs back in, hears a "Sigh" that he interprets as "that of a Man in some Pain" and then "a broken Noise, *as if* of Words half express'd"

(177). When it turns out to be not a man but "a most monstrous frightful old He-goat, just making his Will, as we say, and gasping for Life, and dying indeed of meer old Age," the beast's human attributes give a tragicomic twist to the situation (178). Monstrous and frightful or not, this superannuated old fellow is also a witty emblem of Crusoe's dwindling humanity.

Now, with the old goat out of the way, no obstacles remain to Crusoe's entrenchment. Another passageway leads to yet another cave, deeper and far more grand than the first one. To reach it, Crusoe has to crawl on his hands and knees through a long (almost ten yards), low, and narrow passage. The first time he does so without any light to see by. Then he returns with candles:

When I was got through the Strait, I found the Roof rose higher up, I believe near twenty Foot; but never was such a glorious Sight seen in the Island, I dare say, as it was, to look round the Sides and Roof of this Vault, or Cave; the Walls reflected 100 thousand Lights to me from my two Candles; what it was in Rock, whether Diamonds, or any other precious Stones, or Gold, which I rather suppos'd it to be, I knew not.

(178–179)

The cave within the cave, the womb at the end of the tunnel, turns into a vaulted cathedral full of sparkle and opulence, a stately pleasure-dome and a dazzling rival to the exotic follies and fantasies that dotted the eighteenth-century landscape.

If Crusoe's cave-dwelling anticipates Gulliver's and Uncle Toby's self-enclosing habits of mind, the splendor of his discovery makes one think as well of the elaborate grotto at Twickenham where Pope liked to shine an alabaster lamp and watch the "thousand pointed Rays" that glittered there and were "reflected over the Place."[10] Or of Ralph Ellison's invisible man at the end of his story, holed up in a cellar with myriad light bulbs shining all around. Crusoe, Pope, and invisible man, all of them make or find an indoor universe, full of artificial suns, of which each is sole proprietor, wholly protected from savages, from the corruptions of politics and the city, or from the savagery of American life. All of them, like Crusoe, fancy themselves "like one of the ancient Giants, which are said to live in Caves, and Holes, in the Rocks, where none could come at them" (179). They fantasize a troglodyte innocence.

What does Defoe think of all this? It is no easier to be certain than to know for sure what Swift thinks of Gulliver's retreat to the stables. But there are hints that Crusoe's cave-dwelling strikes Defoe as doubtfully human. It depends on how we read a passage like the one where Crusoe, having found his perfect cave, admits that if he could be sure no savages would disturb him, then he would be content to spend the rest of his days there, "even to the last Moment, till I had laid me down and dy'd, like the old Goat in the Cave" (180). An "old goat," runs the proverb, "is never the more reverend for his beard," and anyone who doubts Defoe's capacity for ironic effects might be convinced by Crusoe's projection of his goatish ending. In any case, he has reached the end of the line, with nothing to do but die or else somehow come to terms with the world. As one of the giants before the flood, as presiding genius of his

[10]Pope to Edward Blount, June 2, 1725, in *The Correspondence of Alexander Pope*, ed. George Sherburn, 5 vols. (Oxford: Clarendon Press, 1956), II: 297. Maynard Mack notices the similarity between Pope's grotto and Crusoe's cave in *The Garden and the City: Retirement and Politics in the Later Poetry of Pope, 1731–1743* (Toronto: University of Toronto Press, 1969), p. 44n.

vast cathedral-universe-cave, he has accomplished his perverse destiny as self-contained, self-containing hero. But
unlike Gulliver or Toby, who live adjacent to the world, he
cannot choose to come to terms. On real desert islands, the
only way back is for the world to come to you. So now
Crusoe climbs his hill one day and sees the cannibals
through his prospective glass. His garrison life is ended, if
not his garrison mentality.

"My Island was now peopled," he says, "and I thought
my self very rich in Subjects; and it was a merry Reflection
which I frequently made, How like a King I look'd" (241).
Like his relentless colonizing of Friday and his casual neg-
lect of him after they finally leave the island, this elabora-
tion of imperial fantasies marks Crusoe as forever an islander, even though he has an occasional glimpse of what it
would be like to make contact with the lost continent. It is
just that imaginary continent, primitive and spontaneous,
that Friday represents. He brings to Crusoe's silent island
exuberant sounds. His tumultuous reunion with his father is
one of Defoe's virtuoso pieces masquerading as plain prose:

> *Friday* kiss'd him, embrac'd him, hugg'd him, cry'd, laugh'd, hol-
> low'd, jump'd about, danc'd, sung, then cry'd again, wrung his
> Hands, beat his own Face, and Head, and then sung, and jump'd
> about again, like a distracted Creature.

For just a moment, Crusoe's and Friday's island manages to
look like a community instead of a kingdom. Even Crusoe is
not immune to its values: "It is not easy for me to express
how it mov'd me to see what Extasy and filial Affection had
work'd in this poor *Savage*, at the Sight of his Father, and of
his being deliver'd from Death" (238). Spontaneous feelings
contest the territory with preacherly moralizing. On the one
hand, unforced "Extasy and filial Affection" and an un-
premeditated, if not fluent, sharing of that feeling; on the

other, reasons and categories—"this poor *Savage*," "at the Sight of his Father," "of his being deliver'd from Death." The measured accents of the moralist ward off the sweep of primitive feelings. Even at the moment of sharpest commitment, Crusoe is still covering up.[11]

Beside *Robinson Crusoe*, *Gulliver's Travels* and *Tristram Shandy* are less comprehensive tracts in the literature of wordlessness. Both are thoroughly secular: nothing in Gulliver's experience or in Uncle Toby's matches Crusoe's discovery of the footstep. But because they are more specialized, they are in ways more accessible. Crusoe's island life is material for biography; Gulliver's adventures, especially those in Laputa and Houyhnhnmland, are material for a case study, as is Toby's seclusion. Imagine that all three characters were real and had had the adventures told about them. Surely we would want to know more about Crusoe than about Gulliver and Toby. It's plausible, therefore, to deal with the two of them, selectively, as clinical cases: the one a despairing philologist, the other a poor innocent whose life is threatened by living in a world where no good answer exists to the importunate question: "Where . . . ?"

Gulliver moves from fluency to blockage, from speech to speechlessness. The breakdown is all the more massive given his special skills. He has had a series of linguistic triumphs. When he arrives at Lilliput, he already knows or has a smattering of "*High* and *Low Dutch*, *Latin*, *French*, *Spanish*, *Italian*, and *Lingua Franca*" (31). He picks up the local

[11]The chapter on solitude in Crusoe's *Serious Reflections* proclaims that he was scarcely ever solitary on the island except in his rare contemplations on sublime things. See *Serious Reflections during the Life and Surprising Adventures of Robinson Crusoe*, Vol. III in Defoe, *Romances and Narratives*, ed. George A. Aitken (London: J. M. Dent, 1899), pp. 1–15. But the deep sense of Crusoe's assertion (p. 15) that we can be solitary anywhere, whether in a city or on an island, confirms the proposition that island life is above all a state of mind.

tongue in about three weeks. The Brodingnagian language, though harder, takes him only a few months. In Laputa, thanks to some careful instruction, he's doing well within hours. In Houyhnhnmland he understands the horses in about ten weeks and is fairly fluent inside of three months. What's more, he fancies himself a scholar:

> THE Word, which I interpret the *Flying* or *Floating Island,* is in the Original *Laputa*; whereof I could never learn the true Etymology. *Lap* in the old obsolete Language signifieth *High,* and *Untuh* a *Governor*; from which they say by Corruption was derived *Laputa* from *Lapuntuh*. But I do not approve of this Derivation, which seems to be a little strained. I ventured to offer to the Learned among them a Conjecture of my own, that *Laputa* was *quasi Lap outed*; *Lap* signifying properly the dancing of the Sun Beams in the Sea; and *outed* a Wing, which however I shall not obtrude, but submit to the judicious Reader.

> (161–162)

But Gulliver, the modest philologue, has been corrupted by Laputian habits of mind, and this preposterous etymologizing shows him on the downhill road to speechlessness. About the etymology of Laputa not much can be said: between the accepted derivation and Gulliver's alternative, there's nothing to choose. Like the island itself, these derivations float above the earth unanchored to any linguistic context and are hopelessly far-fetched. Beneath the surface of Swift's philological satire lies the suspicion, which Gulliver translates into belief, that in matters of language we serve the lord of misrule.

It is in Book III that the reader realizes how much attention Swift has paid all along to such matters, though it has been mainly playful attention so far. Now the line between playfulness and the anarchy of infantile regression is crossed and (we think) perhaps for good, the outcome hanging in the balance until we come to Houyhnhnmland. Lagado looks like a playground gone mad. Not only do the

virtuosi dabble, childlike, in excrement, they want to restore
men to a nonverbal state:

THE first Project was to shorten Discourse by cutting Polysylla-
bles into one, and leaving out Verbs and Participles; because in
Reality all things imaginable are but Nouns.

(185)

It is a wonderfully scrambled picture theory of language:
"because in Reality all things imaginable are but Nouns."
What does "in Reality" mean? Gulliver seems to be saying,
colloquially, nothing more than "really." Still we can hardly
help taking "in" as a genuine locative and placing reality
somewhere, out there, in an external world that is the natural habitat of things. Yet these things turn out to be furniture of the mind: "all things imaginable." The clause
breaks at the middle, the first part ("because in Reality all
things") offering an apparently substantial world, the second ("all things imaginable are but Nouns") overlapping
the first and sabotaging its solidity. Because things are capable of being *named*, it is in one sense a tautology to say that
"all things imaginable are but Nouns"; but in a supervening
sense it dissolves the reality of the external world to reduce
everything to verbal constructions. The gap between "out
there" and "in here" is huge because of, not despite, the
overlapping structure. The relationship between language
and what it aims to represent turns out to be a pious fancy,
as the linguistic texture of verbs and participles falls away.
Nothing remains but things and things imagined, object and
subject, real world and uncreating word. It is a bleak business, and Gulliver has been touched by the general madness (he is nothing if not suggestible). No wonder, as we
will learn in Book IV, that he is in danger of schizophrenic
withdrawal.

In the School of Languages at Lagado, the road is open to

silence. The projectors' second scheme follows from the first:

> THE other, was a Scheme for entirely abolishing all Words whatsoever: And this was urged as a great Advantage in Point of Health as well as Brevity. For, it is plain, that every Word we speak is in some Degree a Diminution of our Lungs by Corrosion; and consequently contributes to the shortning of our Lives. An Expedient was therefore offered, that since Words are only Names for *Things*, it would be more convenient for all Men to carry about them, such *Things* as were necessary to express the particular Business they are to discourse on.
>
> (185)

The scheme convinces the learned and wise, if not the "common People," and many of them adopt it—with "only this Inconvenience," that the greater and the more various a man's business, the larger the bundle of things he has to carry, unless he can afford a servant or two to help. Since the learned and wise aren't always rich, scenes ensue that might have come from Samuel Beckett:

> I have often beheld two of those Sages almost sinking under the Weight of their Packs, like Pedlars among us; who when they met in the Streets would lay down their Loads, open their Sacks, and hold Conversation for an Hour together; then put up their Implements, help each other to resume their Burthens, and take their Leave.
>
> (185–186)

Like Crusoe or Beckett's people, these sages are technocrats, and every metaphor has become excruciatingly literal. Laying down one's load and taking up one's burden are customary metaphors of spiritual life reduced to the physical. A deflected and mechanical sexuality colors the comic scene: to "hold Conversation . . . together" toys with the other meaning of conversation, laying down one's load and opening up one's sack become sudden sexual parodies, putting up one's implements serves as an image of release, no sooner accomplished than the burden has to be taken up once more. The literal flowers wildly into metaphor again, asserting drives both of body and mind in a fantasy—one might almost call it pornographic—of dehumanization. Crusoe's buried sexuality, Uncle Toby's wounded sexuality, and the conversation of the sages: all are symptoms of the island life. Perhaps the way has even been prepared for Gulliver's curious equine tastes at the end of his travels. Around Swift's parody of nominalism, witty and urbane, hover the dark angels of despair.

Corresponding to the nonverbal forms of life proposed in the School of Languages is the machine designed to produce "a compleat Body of all Arts and Sciences" (184). In the one case language dies out as it is absorbed in the furnishings of the external world; in the other it dies out as it is absorbed in a system of random self-reference that robs it of its roots in experience. Both processes follow from the assumption that language is a closed system. The picture of the machine makes the point better (so the joke seems to be) than a thousand words.

The picture confronts and challenges Gulliver's meticulous verbal description, which manages to make the machine sound almost plausible. We learn that the thing is twenty feet square and placed in the middle of the room, that it is put together with wood and wires and paper, and that on the paper pasted to each square are "all the Words of their Language in their several Moods, Tenses, and Declensions, but without any Order" (184). In a receptive mood, we might not even notice the fallacy of "all the Words" and think, why not? But the picture emphasizes the craziness of bounding language in a nutshell. The machine looks like nothing so much as a rack to twist and torture language into

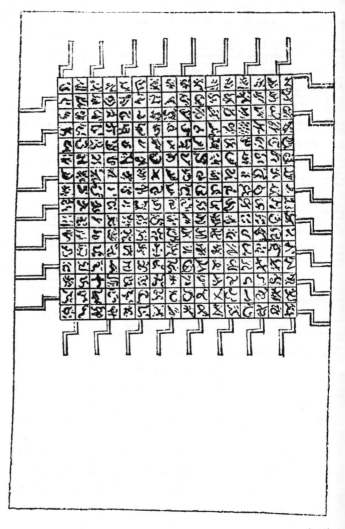

(183)

doing the projector's will before giving up the ghost altogether. Once the "Body" of arts and sciences is complete, language will have done what it can do; the machine will be obsolete and ready for the junkpile. After so much adverse conditioning to the word, Gulliver's final retreat to the silence of the stables could almost have been predicted. It is the final step of the process begun among the projectors, sages, flappers, and virtuosi.

To be sure, Gulliver claims at the end of his travels to be conversing with his two stone-horses: they "understand me," he says, "tolerably well" (290). But Mary Gulliver's lament, done up by Pope with saucy vulgarity, throws a different light on Gulliver's equine conversations and his friendship with the groom who, next to the horses, is his "greatest Favourite":

> Why then that dirty Stable-boy thy Care?
> What mean those Visits to the *Sorrel Mare*?
> ("Mary Gulliver to Captain Lemuel Gulliver," lines 29–30)

Pope misremembers some of the facts—Gulliver has sadly left the sorrel nag (who's not a mare) behind in Houyhnhnmland—but it is the joke and its implications that count:

> Forth in the Street I rush with frantick Cries:
> The Windows open; all the Neighbours rise:
> *Where sleeps my* Gulliver? *O tell me where?*
> The Neighbours answer, *With the Sorrel Mare.*
> (lines 45–48)

Gulliver's conversings reflect his yearning for a form of life free from language. This yearning, which he brings with him to Houyhnhnmland, conditions his experience there from the start.

What needs emphasis is that the Houyhnhnms seem not to use language in any sense we can understand; rather they

neigh and whinny and make the usual horsy sounds. It is
Gulliver who interprets these sounds as words. After being
rescued from the Yahoos by the gray horse who will be his
master, he almost immediately decides that variations of
cadence in the horse's neighing indicate that something
more is going on than would meet our ears—"I almost
began to think he was speaking to himself in some Language of his own" (225). Criteria of probability matter here
as they do not anywhere else in the *Travels*: it would simply
not occur to most of us to assume what Gulliver does.
Whether we think him sane or insane is unimportant.
Whatever the diagnosis, he would like to leave the forms of
human speech behind. The wish fulfills itself.

Human language and Houyhnhnm language are incompatible. That is what lies behind the uncomprehending
response of Gulliver's master to his tale of coming to
Houyhnhnmland in a great hollow vessel:

> It was with some Difficulty, and by the Help of many Signs, that I
> brought him to understand me. He replied, That I must needs be
> mistaken, or that I *said the thing which was not*. (For they have no
> Word in their Language to express Lying or Falshood.) He knew it
> was impossible that there could be a Country beyond the Sea, or
> that a Parcel of Brutes could move a wooden Vessel whither they
> pleased upon Water. He was sure no *Houyhnhnm* alive could make
> such a Vessel, or would trust *Yahoos* to manage it.
>
> (235)

From this side of the sea, the explanation seems not merely
true but probable. To the Houyhnhnms it is impossible.
Among the things that his master can't concede, because he
can't understand it, is that Gulliver might speak a language
of his own, any more than we can imagine that the neighing
of horses or the beeping of dolphins fully constitutes what
we call language. We are like Gulliver's master ourselves,

knowing there could be no Houyhnhnmland beyond the sea: metaphorically, the sea is that of human language. Would we ever want to accuse a talking horse, or Robinson Crusoe's parrot, of lying? At most we would want to tell them that they had said the thing which is not, just as Gulliver's master tells him.

That odd formula, one of the most teasing and finally exasperating things in the *Travels*, defies precise construction, but it evidently denies Gulliver the terms of his own experience. "To say the thing" is to call something into being. "To say the thing which is not" is to have the ground cut away by the paradox of negation. As if a magician had waved his wand and said "Presto," the great hollow vessel, Gulliver's companions, the country beyond the sea, and the language of the country beyond the sea all vanish without a trace. The demands of the satire and of the story require Gulliver's master to have a change of heart, as he does a few pages further on. If he did not, there would be no more to say, or at least nothing that could be said to us, Gulliver's nonexistent readers. Gulliver at least has evidence to suppose he exists, but what risks are waiting for him when he is thrown out of Houyhnhnmland and has to go back to England? Might he not tumble back into nonexistence? His silent conversations with his horses aim to stabilize a precarious identity; his gingerly reconciliation with the Yahoos is a daring effort to go back across a large divide.

Compared to Crusoe and Gulliver, Uncle Toby, with his rood and a half of ground, is more lovable but also a sadder instance. In his bowling green, his paradise of covertly innocent sexuality regained, he finds a place to hide:

It was sheltered from a house . . . by a tall yew hedge, and was covered on the other three sides, from mortal sight, by rough holly and thickset flowering shrubs;—so that the idea of not being seen, did not a little contribute to the idea of pleasure pre-conceived in my uncle *Toby*'s mind.

                                                                    (98–99)

What Toby, like Gulliver, is hiding from is language, especially the awful difficulties he has in telling his story. His struggles, like those in "greater THEATRES" (87) that arise from confused and indeterminate meanings, bring on "sharp paroxisms and exacerbations of his wound" (83). They are literally killing him: " 'Twas not by ideas,—by heaven! his life was put in jeopardy by words" (87). But Trim hopes that if Toby will silently reenact a less threatening war, it will cure him, and Toby heads for the bowling green with all the "heat and expectation" of a lover going to his mistress (98). Like Crusoe and Gulliver, he withdraws into wordless invisibility.

To be sure, Sterne sidles up to the possibility of Toby's actual recovery. Crusoe hardly knows he is sick, despite all his clamorous prayers and penitences. Gulliver does know it, but the prognosis is bad. Though he has begun by the end to eat with his wife and though he "permits" her "to answer (but with the utmost Brevity) the few Questions I asked her," still he's talking a language different from hers (295). Who needs permission to answer a question? Words still do not mean to Gulliver what they mean to us. One would not want to bet on his recovery. But Toby is different: "My uncle *Toby fell in love.*" And his falling in love allows Tristram temporarily to extricate both of them from the labyrinth of verbal definitions:

—'TWILL come out of itself by and bye.—All I contend for is, that I am not *obliged* to set out with a definition of what love is; and so long as I can go on with my story intelligibly, with the help of the word itself, without any other idea to it, than what I have in common with the rest of the world, why should I differ from it a moment before the time? —When I can get no further,—and find myself entangled on all sides of this mystick labyrinth,—my Opinion will then come in, in course,—and lead me out.

At present, I hope I shall be sufficiently understood, in telling the reader, my uncle *Toby fell in love.*

Not that Tristram altogether likes the locution: if we fall in love, that seems to mean it "is a thing *below* a man," and Tristram thinks that an unworthy notion (which he fathers on Plato but might have fathered on, say, Rabelais). But he doesn't linger over these doubts: "Let love therefore be what it will,—my uncle *Toby* fell into it" (469). It looks for the moment as if Toby has been rescued from both the embarrassments of language and his isolation. Maybe feelings can rescue man from his islands. In these dramas of isolation the stage is set for the evangelical message of a sexless sentimentalism. Yet sentimentalism—and Sterne knew this—was the worship of feeling deflected back on itself. *Tristram Shandy* is no less an island drama than *Robinson Crusoe*. No sooner has Toby fallen in love than a doubtfulness more disabling than before floods in.[12] It comes not just from the fact of Toby's wound but because the puzzles and betrayals of language plague us more than ever when we try to return from island life. The gospel of salvation through feeling runs up against the fact that some feelings will never be communicated and some things never told. Toby's rescue and cure are illusory; the waters close in when the Widow Wadman wants to know everything there is to know about his wound.

The widow realizes it is a touchy subject; she circles around it, asking Dr. Slop whether Toby is "ever likely to recover of his wound—?" (636). Slop's reply, that he is

[12]In a forthcoming essay, John Traugott argues vigorously that sentiment was in fact, for Sterne, the way out.

recovered, makes matters worse, since neither the widow nor we know exactly what Toby has to recover from, or how recovery might be defined. The definition of love has come in the back door, even though the widow regards it as an operational, not a metaphysical matter: "But what do you mean by a recovery? Mrs. *Wadman* would say." This is the beginning of the end. Dr. Slop being "the worst man alive at definitions," the widow can only get what she needs to know from Toby (637). Things come full circle as she frames her delicate question: "And whereabouts, dear Sir, quoth Mrs. *Wadman*, a little categorically, did you receive this sad blow?" The answer, as Toby demonstrates on the map that he quickly sends Corporal Trim in search of, is: "before the gate of St. *Nicolas*, in one of the traverses of the trench, opposite to the salient angle of the demi-bastion of St. *Roch*" (638). What could be more circumstantial, more exquisitely precise? Toby's habit of mind mimics that of the silent sages or of Crusoe, the great collector. Circumstantial realism, elaborate detail, careful enumeration, all of them are island substitutes for definitions which, alas for Toby and the widow, do turn out to matter. The two of them are farther from each other than before, though Toby does not know what has happened. If Crusoe finds a noble savage who acts out before his eyes the spontaneous motions of instinctive life, if Gulliver makes some gestures of accommodation with his wife and family, Toby's expansive act of falling in love merely defeats itself. His is the saddest, though also the most tough-minded, story of them all.

My reason for pointing toward Ford Madox Ford's *The Good Soldier*, "the saddest story" as Ford's original title had it, is associational; but the association can be drawn out. The stiff-upper-lip wordlessness of Ford's Edward Ashburnham, the latent cruelties and violence of Dowell's story, its themes of impotence and of a paradise, however fanciful, associated with the sun and olive groves of Provence, all these are quite startling points of contact between Ford's novel and *Tristram Shandy*. So is the theme of voyeurism, which is the one strand still to be separated from the fabric of these island lives. Ford's narrator is more watcher than watched: in him the artist figure absorbs the *isolato*. It is a later stage of the process that we are watching at its start. Crusoe and Gulliver and Toby are more spied upon than spying. Their stories emphasize the presence on our islands of tourists, spies, voyeurs coming through.

This is especially the case with poor Uncle Toby. Even as he savors the thought of being invisible, the narrator's voice breaks in to say it can't be so:

Vain thought! however thick it was planted about,—or private soever it might seem,—to think, dear uncle *Toby*, of enjoying a thing which took up a whole rood and a half of ground,—and not have it known!

(99)

Mrs. Wadman's house and garden adjoin Toby's garden, and love-militant sets her spying on him and sabotaging his serene encampment. She observes his "motions," is "mistress likewise of his councils of war," and because he innocently welcomes her into his island domain, she comes to the door of his sentry-box; in fact—ultimate violation —she sometimes "endeavour[s] to blow my uncle *Toby* up in the very sentry-box itself" (552). Salvation through love and feeling means welcoming a traitor into the garden.

But at least Mrs. Wadman is known, more or less, for what she is and what she wants. The more sinister intruder is the prescient narrator. As the ambidexter who sets these events in motion, he violates the sanctuary of his characters the moment he creates it. Crusoe's island, Gulliver's stables,

Toby's fantasyland—they all resemble those models of caves or dungeons made to show curious tourists what the real thing is like: good imitations if you ignore the fact that one wall isn't there. Of this both Defoe and Swift have some knowledge. Homer O. Brown's notion that the mysterious footprint can be taken as Defoe's signature, the evidence of an authorial presence, is alluring;[13] and Swift was endlessly aware of himself as involved in what he created. But again it is Sterne who knows best what it means to be the creator of guarded selves. To be his characters' destiny is to betray them by his knowledge:

> THE Fates, who certainly all foreknew of these amours of widow *Wadman* and my uncle *Toby*, had, from the first creation of matter and motion (and with more courtesy than they usually do things of this kind) established such a chain of causes and effects hanging so fast to one another, that it was scarce possible for my uncle *Toby* to have dwelt in any other house in the world, or to have occupied any other garden in *Christendom*, but the very house and garden which join'd and laid parallel to Mrs. *Wadman's* . . . .
>
> (552)

The self-consciousness of the modern author reflects the stratagems of mind assuaging its loneliness by creating other people to share with wholly rather than in part—or as the island analogy would have it, not at all. Still the experience is shared at a distance, as the fates share in our lives. This cool and regressive voyeurism makes Toby's isolation more complete in the long run. The fates work by intermediaries, using one person as another's destiny. Mrs. Wadman peeps in on Toby, Tristram watches Mrs. Wadman watching Toby, Sterne (somewhere) watches Tristram watching Mrs. Wadman watching Toby. Though we feel

---

[13]"The Displaced Self in the Novels of Daniel Defoe," *ELH*, 38 (1971): 583ff. I am simplifying Brown's analysis, a part of his subtle study of "radical egocentricity" (p. 565) in Defoe's fiction.

close to Toby, we are far from him too. The roles of reader and author coalesce in frustration. Everyone gets caught in this warren of enclosures, sentry-boxes, and guarded selves.

If the progress from *Robinson Crusoe* and *Gulliver's Travels* to *Tristram Shandy* is toward an increasing authorial self-consciousness, it is also, as regards Uncle Toby, toward a constriction of boundaries. Crusoe imagines himself, at first, as emperor of all he surveys, and even his cave is very grand; Gulliver, though he goes to many strange lands, always ends up in domesticity; Toby, not content with the self-imposed limits of his playground, makes himself a sentry-box. One speculates that a law, or something like it, is at work: that as boundaries contract, authorial self-consciousness increases. The next chapter, dealing with even narrower confinements than these, deals as well with a variety of turnkeys and warders. Their presence lends weight to the speculation.

III

Prisons, Pastorals, and Warders

GEORGES POULET distinguishes between the good and bad cosmic consciousness of the eighteenth century: the one ponders "the circle and the center of the solar universe, which it thinks to possess by thought"; the other "searches for the center and the circle of the total universe, and finds them nowhere." The good consciousness, at its best, leads to the elegant spider web of subjectivity or to the Platonic aesthetic of the circle, as reconstructed by the likes of Joseph Addison or Bernardin de Saint Pierre. The bad consciousness, at its worst, leads to paralysis in the presence of infinity: "The apparent center, the first point of view where one had placed oneself, seems less a starting point than a fast ground, from where, no more than the swan of Mallarmé, one may fly."[1] Though the normal situation is less one of polar opposition than of mixed feelings, this division

[1] *The Metamorphoses of the Circle*, trans. Carley Dawson and Elliott Coleman in collaboration with the author (Baltimore: Johns Hopkins Press, 1966), p. 63.

of the territory of consciousness into good and bad is a useful categorical distinction for sorting out fictional confinements of the age.

There are happy prisons and good consciousness in (for example) *Moll Flanders, Tom Jones,* and *Roderick Random*—happy, that is, in the events they prepare the way for. In these novels, the hero's ritual descent into the hell of Newgate, the Gatehouse, or the Marshalsea means a return to the center of the universe of self, conceived not on the subjective model of spider-consciousness at the center of its web but as life in action—its purpose, once the center has been found, being to get on with it, and its reward being the recovery of an idyllic world. These novels rest on the myth of the past recaptured and birthrights regained. They are fictions of "captivity" and "deliverance." Like Addison's aesthetics of the circle, they restore a lost world by an act of will. This act of recovery brings the artist more decisively than before into the net of his own creation, but even his ambiguous presence does not undermine the viability of the world that has been recaptured.

If there are some happy prisons, there are also some fast grounds—confinements without compensatory elations, that produce near-paralysis if not claustrophobia and terror. These confinements, both of body and mind, find their most powerful representation in Richardson's *Clarissa*, the novel that more than any other has defined the physical and mental space of modern fiction.[2] But other texts, on a smaller scale, display similar feelings, sometimes with a

[2]For discussions of confinement in *Clarissa*, see Leo Braudy, "Penetration and Impenetrability in *Clarissa*," in *New Approaches to Eighteenth-Century Literature: Selected Papers from the English Institute*, ed. Phillip Harth (New York: Columbia University Press, 1974), pp. 177–206; and Max Byrd, "The Madhouse, the Whorehouse, and the Convent" (see Chap. I, above, note 20.)

proportional strength of expression: on the one hand, for example, Swift's city poems and Defoe's *Journal of the Plague Year*, all representing London as sealed off from the countryside, allowing neither escape nor entry, enforcing eerie stillness or wild spasmodic motion; on the other hand, a poem like John Dyer's *Grongar Hill* or Pope's much grander *Eloisa to Abelard*, both of them set in a pastoral landscape but perceptually at a remove from it. Though nothing could seem further from Dyer's leisured elegance than the frenzied autoeroticism of Pope's poem, the perceptual passivity of the one reciprocates the claustral furies of the other, just as the immobilities of Swift's "Morning" reciprocate the apocalyptic but enclosed motions of the "City Shower" or of Defoe's *Journal*. Each in its separate way tells of entrapment. And when the figure of the poet-narrator appears from the wings at the end of *Eloisa to Abelard*, we may feel cheated. Wasn't it, we want to ask, more serious a business than this?

But if there were happy prisons and fast grounds, paradises regained and others lost, were there no mediations between them? No one to adjust the claims of good consciousness and bad? What Swift does in *A Tale of a Tub* is not only to station himself, ironically, between the giddy heights of elation and a secure but restrictive ground, but at the same time—narrowly, by a last-minute wave of the wand—to reconcile the contradictory senses of confinement as death-dealing and conclusive, initiatory and life-giving. What John Gay does in the "Newgate pastoral" that he called *The Beggar's Opera* is to incorporate the lost world of pastoral fertility inside the walls of Newgate and—more decisively than Swift, though also at the last moment—to assert the generative powers of the prison. Less metaphysically inclined than Swift, Gay does not trouble himself much about the cosmos: *The Beggar's Opera* has no heights but the gallows, no depths but those of Newgate, and is less vertiginous by far than the *Tale*. Only the motto of the play hints at emptiness. But it is wholly an indoor piece, the actual experience of which, after the murk of Swift's city morning or the gloomy shadows of the convent of the Paraclete, is like coming onto an open plain.

Happy prisons, being less subtly interesting than their melancholic counterparts, needn't detain us long. They are actual, not metaphorical, and signify that the good consciousness does not need to veil itself. Moll Flanders is taken, sent to Newgate, tried and convicted for stealing two pieces of brocade, sentenced to die, stirred to repentance. Tom Jones goes to the Gatehouse for having (supposedly) dispatched Mr. Fitzpatrick. Roderick Random goes to the Marshalsea for debt. It is the moment when, as the linear movement of the plot temporarily ceases, things begin to come together. It is predictable, cheerfully formulaic.

Newgate is Moll's home; she was born there. She comes back to find not only her Lancashire husband, destined now to be her husband finally and in earnest, but also a reasonable substitute for the mother who left her to make her picaresque way in the world. Whether we should take her repentance seriously or not as a religious experience, she does in any case recover her powers of feeling. Seeing her Lancashire husband, "I was overwhelm'd with grief for him; my own Case gave me no disturbance compar'd to this . . . in a word, I was perfectly chang'd, and become another Body" (281). Becoming another body, the natural mode of conversion, means in Moll's case entering into the experience of another. It also means the rebirth of relationship. Her governess, that ambiguous nurse, protectress, temptress, and receiver of stolen goods, whom Moll has learned early (and strangely) to call Mother, turns out to have a fair claim to the name: "I sent for my old Governess, and she, *give her her due*, acted the Part of a true Friend." But more than just the part of a true friend. When the news comes that the jury has brought the bill against Moll for felony and burglary, "my Governess acted a true Mother to me, she pittied me, she cryed with me, and for me . . . ." To be sure, Moll's case looks hopeless; "she cou'd not help me; and to add to the Terror of it, 'twas the Discourse all over the House, that I should die for it" (282). The prospect of death, however, accompanies rebirth and the recovery of a lost mother. In *Moll Flanders* Newgate does not inhibit life and motion: though a hellish cauldron of activity, it is womb rather than dungeon. If there's an entrance to hell, there's also a way out. Though linear movement has stopped for the time being, Newgate is an open space, a staging area. The reprieve from death and the substitute sentence of transportation follow naturally. Newgate opens out onto the green world.

The same design is at work in *Tom Jones* and, less emphatically, in *Roderick Random*. Not only does the incarceration of the hero precede release into new life, but in each case self-confrontation points, however tentatively and comically, to new forms of self-understanding. Tom Jones' passing horror that he has committed incest is farcically equivalent and functionally parallel to Moll's rediscovering a mother: Tom has come back to—one hesitates but succumbs to a punning temptation—the waters of his birth as well as to the very center of his own story, the events at the inn at Upton. In *Roderick Random*, though the prison episode has less vital work to do, still it intimates recovery of lost origins and a stirring of new sympathies.

In the Marshalsea, Roderick comes on the startling figure

of Melopoyn, who emerges from a horde of "naked miserable wretches," looking for all the world like an Old Testament prophet or an anchorite who has wandered out of his time: "A figure appeared, wrapped in a dirty rug, tied about his loins with two pieces of list, of different colours, knotted together; having a black bushy beard, and his head covered with a huge mass of brown periwig, which seemed to have been ravished from the crown of some scare-crow" (II: 238). This Gothic apparition, Smollett's grotesque self-recreation, turns out to be a father of sorts, a poet who stirs in Roderick an uncharacteristic urge to clothe the naked and feed the hungry: he sends Melopoyn a bundle of clothes, invites him to dinner, and maybe best of all hears out his story, which comes to an end with a lavish outpouring of gratitude for Roderick's "uncommon benevolence" (II: 268). Being Roderick, it is uncommon in every sense. And it is appropriate, even witty, that the self-parodic artist draws warmth and sustenance from Roderick Random, Smollett's first fictional offspring. Having acknowledged a projected image of the person who fictionally fathered him, like Moll discovering that her substitute mother can truly act the part (that is to say, can bring her to life), or even like Tom believing for a time that he's slept with his mother, Roderick has performed a rite of passage: he has come to terms with the insecurity of lost parentage and is ready for new journeys out.

At the same time, we shouldn't overestimate the comic "logic" of these novels. The mood, at the end of them, is exactly one of release, therefore of exhilaration. The happy endings that the prison interlude prepares for are doubly happy because everything might have turned out for the worst. And though in fact it turns out for the best, that is more happenstance than a matter of overarching comic form or the inevitability of character; just as, conversely, Clarissa's tragedy is gratuitous. (Even if there's always something Clarissa prefers to truth, do we believe she deserved her fate?) In the literature of incarceration, even of "happy" prisons, causes are tenuously linked to effects. The feelings of being set loose that accompany last-minute reprieves reflect our suspicion that only a lucky cast of the dice has averted disaster. Or even that we have cheated the gallows, as Moll does. It is not so much a matter of rights and wrongs but simply of what, if it were us, we'd want to happen. For the outcome, we have to depend on Fortune.

But Fortune, in a fictional setting, is another name for the author. If the literature of incarceration portrays a world of uncertain causality, that means the author takes increasing responsibility for the destiny of his characters. Fielding, in particular, makes the most of this life-and-death power at the same time as he mounts a rear-guard action in defense of "probability": "But to bring our Favourites out of their present Anguish and Distress, and to land them at last on the Shore of Happiness, seems a much harder Task"— harder, that is, than for a tragic writer who could have done everything in a jiffy—"a Task indeed so hard that we do not undertake to execute it." That is, either Tom will get out of his predicament in a "natural" way or not at all. With this sportive denial of omniscience, Fielding draws out the tragicomic possibilities—"If our Reader delights in seeing Executions, I think he ought not to lose any Time in taking a first Row at *Tyburn*"—and tips the reader the wink as well (875). As for the other tragic possibility than threatens Tom and Sophia—that is, the final and necessary parting between author and readers—Fielding meets it straight on: "And now, my Friend, I take this Opportunity (as I shall have no other) of heartily wishing thee well" (913–914). By facing it squarely, he salvages what he can from an awkward situation. It is not the best of all possible worlds where the author has to play so large a part, making his antic motions and then fading from sight, but it is not the worst either —and we aren't wrong to take our releases and exhilarations where we can. That attitude, implicit in fictions like *Moll Flanders* or *Roderick Random*, is quite explicit in the unique case of *Tom Jones*.

If the happy prison opens onto the green world and if the author, in these fictions, plays benevolent despot, the fast ground is shut off from the green world—the author sharing in the experience as passive spectator or wounded captive or both. Of this experience the city becomes the governing symbol; and one way to get a feeling for Swift's and Defoe's London is first by recalling the telegram that seals off Oran in Camus' novel: "Déclarez l'état de peste. Fermez la ville."[3] What is literal in Defoe and Camus—the plague—is figurative in Swift. The city of his "Description of the Morning" is deathlike; the city of his "City Shower," filthy and pestilential. And there is no getting out. Where Swift is at his bleakest—in *Gulliver*, for example, if not in *A Modest Proposal*—an undercurrent of levity turns the whole into something less grim than it might have been or might seem to be. Where he is at his most cheerful, or cheerfully satiric, a basic pessimism exerts its strong contrary drag. In the case of the city poems, this pessimism lies in a perception of the modern city as shut off from the country and, as a self-enclosed parody of the enclosed pastoral life, entirely antithetical to it.

What is most striking about the "Description of the Morning" is the way it suspends motion and falls away into silence. It has little of the movement and bustle and coming alive expected of the morning:

[3] Albert Camus, *La Peste* (Paris: Gallimard, 1947, 1963), p. 77.

Now hardly here and there an Hackney-Coach
Appearing, show'd the Ruddy Morns Approach.
Now *Betty* from her Masters Bed had flown,
And softly stole to discompose her own.
The Slipshod Prentice from his Masters Door,
Had par'd the Dirt, and Sprinkled round the Floor.
Now *Moll* had whirl'd her Mop with dext'rous Airs,
Prepar'd to Scrub the Entry and the Stairs.
The Youth with Broomy Stumps began to trace
The Kennel-Edge, where Wheels had worn the Place.
The Smallcoal-Man was heard with Cadence deep,
'Till drown'd in Shriller Notes of Chimney-Sweep,
Duns at his Lordships Gate began to meet,
And Brickdust *Moll* had Scream'd through half the Street.
The Turnkey now his Flock returning sees,
Duly let out a Nights to Steal for Fees.
The watchful Bailiffs take their silent Stands,
And School-Boys lag with Satchels in their Hands.

Swift's habitual tricks with tenses generate the stillness, as if
time had come to a stop.[4] This is the moment the language
has no name for: when nighttime darkness intersects with
daylight. But the stillness of it yields a twilight mood.
Things, people, and even the personification of morning
are frozen in place. The promise contained in the word
"appearing"—"Now hardly here and there an Hackney-
Coach / Appearing"—is unfulfilled as present dissolves into
past, "show'd the Ruddy Morns Approach." Really the
morning does not approach; its approach has been passive-
ly "shown." And the action of the poem recedes farther
into the past as the frozen moment stretches out: "Now
Betty from her Masters Bed had flown"; the prentice
"had par'd the Dirt"; Moll "had whirl'd her Mop"; and,

[4]The effect resembles that in Swift's "The Day of Judgement," where a
rapid and unsettling shifting of tenses creates the illusion of experience
outside temporal limits.

after a curious return to the past and a venture into the passive, "Brickdust *Moll* had Scream'd through half the Street." She has, as it were, the other half of the street still to go. Her scream is stopped; there is silence. Only now the poem moves into the present tense, not as an image of process but of its absence:

> The Turnkey now his Flock returning sees,
> Duly let out a Nights to Steal for Fees.
> The watchful Bailiffs take their silent Stands,
> And School-Boys lag with Satchels in their Hands.

Turnkey and bailiffs preside over the stillness. The turnkey, parodic shepherd and parodic Christ, as well as an embryonic artist-watcher, frames "his Flock returning" within the act of seeing them. Verbally and visually the little flock is trapped, captive before any lock is turned on them. Meanwhile, bailiffs watch boys on their way to school, and the boys hang back. The syllables of the last line stretch out; the satchels weigh the schoolboys down, they never do get to school. The poem is a study in arrested motion.

If the "Description of the Morning" comes to a dead stop, the "City Shower" comes to a crescendo of movement; but it turns out to be a recycling, not a purgation, and the storm brings the normal life of the city to a standstill. Everyone scurries and squeezes into shelter. Women crowd into shops pretending they're going to buy. Law students, seamstresses, Whigs and Tories, jostle together. It is as if someone had speeded up a film projector just before the end of the reel. Funniest spectacle of all is the beau in his sedan chair:

> Box'd in a Chair the Beau impatient sits,
> While Spouts run clatt'ring o'er the Roof by Fits. . . .
>   (lines 43–44)

But, funny as he is, fear and suppressed aggression live at
the heart of the experience:

> And ever and anon with frightful Din
> The Leather sounds, he trembles from within.
> So when *Troy* Chair-men bore the Wooden Steed,
> Pregnant with *Greeks*, impatient to be freed,
> (Those Bully *Greeks*, who, as the Moderns do,
> Instead of paying Chair-men, run them thro'.)
> *Laoco'n* struck the Outside with his Spear,
> And each imprison'd Hero quak'd for Fear.
>
> (lines 45–52)

The simile conjures up a mysterious mock-epic plot, as the
trapped beau suddenly turns into a conspiratorial figure.
What is he plotting against? The citadel? Or the forces of
the natural world that trap him, yet challenge him to come
out? This conspiratorial image touches all the trapped people of the city contagiously. We see them as vaguely furtive.
The violence of the external world stirs up spasmodic
countermotions: each imprisoned hero quakes for fear.

Only the poet, a reluctant parody of Lear on the heath,
avoids furtiveness and scurrying:

> Ah! where must needy Poet seek for Aid,
> When Dust and Rain at once his Coat invade;
> His only Coat, where Dust confus'd with Rain,
> Roughen the Nap, and leave a mingled Stain.
>
> (lines 27–30)

There is no answer: we imagine the poet as enduring the
storm and telling its mock-apocalyptic tale. It is a witty
version of the artist as privileged seer, paying the price for
his special insight. But in fact he is caught like everybody
else. The city that shuts out the light in the "Description of
the Morning" sets the limits of experience in the "City
Shower." The drama is reflexive, the poet a perceiving eye,
the city a body with veins and sinews:

> Now from all Parts the swelling Kennels flow,
> And bear their Trophies with them as they go:
> Filth of all Hues and Odours seem to tell
> What Street they sail'd from, by their Sight and Smell.
> They, as each Torrent drives, with rapid Force
> From *Smithfield*, or St. *Pulchre*'s shape their Course,
> And in huge Confluent join at *Snow-Hill* Ridge,
> Fall from the *Conduit* prone to *Holborn-Bridge*.
> Sweepings from Butchers Stalls, Dung, Guts, and Blood, ⎫
> Drown'd Puppies, stinking Sprats, all drench'd in Mud, ⎬
> Dead Cats and Turnip-Tops come tumbling down the Flood. ⎭
>
>   (lines 53–63)

This flood of dung, guts, and blood seeks a sea it never finds. The tumultuous motion of the final triplet leads nowhere. Far from being merely a parody of Dryden, the triplet consumes itself in a frustration of natural process—that is, the process of the couplet: the twice-repeated rhyme signifies blockage. A closed system, the city circulates and recirculates its offal, feeds on its excrement. But even though the storm is mock-apocalypse and mock-purification, still it might sweep us along with it. If the flood has a destination, we and the poet are it. The metropolis, *c'est nous*. Like everyone else we had better take shelter.

The feelings thus wittily stated and controlled in Swift's city poems take on fierce intensity in *A Journal of the Plague Year*, an epic of confinement and surveillance that turns on the decision to seal off the city by shutting up infected houses and setting neighbor against neighbor, the one as watchman of the other. The narrator H. F. (like other writers on the subject)[5] disapproves, believing "that the shutting up of Houses thus by Force, and restraining, or rather imprisoning People in their own Houses . . . was of little or no Service in the Whole." Shutting people up makes them

[5]For background, see *A Journal of the Plague Year*, ed. Landa (see Texts Cited), p. 267n.

want to break out, and, having broken out, then they have
no place to go: "Nay, I am of Opinion, it was rather hurtful,
having forc'd those desperate People to wander abroad with
the Plague upon them, who would otherwise have died
quietly in their Beds" (71). The plague reassumes metaphorical force as a desperate wandering. In the intensified
laboratory conditions that it creates, H. F. begins to see his
way to something like a general psychology of confinement.

Wherever he looks, he discovers violence, irrationality,
panic, fear, hatred of others. The killing of watchmen (some
eighteen or twenty of them) is the least of it. More subtle
and symptomatic is that those who escape go about infect-
ing others, leading to the belief "that it was natural to the
infected People to desire to infect others." This, says H. F.,
was "really false," but his understanding has not carried
him all the way into the dark places of his own laboratory
(70). If the plague is contagious, so is the shutting up of
houses. Breaking out of an infected house spreads the
plague, and other houses will have to be shut up, too. Is it
really false to think of breaking out as wanting to spread the
sickness? At the same time, there is nothing else to do but
try to break out; that is the psychology of entrapment. H. F.
sees this, and this is why he disapproves of shutting up the
infected houses. The force that shuts people up is also what
"forc'd those desperate People to wander abroad with the
Plague upon them." External force begets an internal counterforce. Who would not, given the chance, have to break
out of an infected house?

The *Journal* swings back and forth between the extremes
of stillness and the frenetic movement of a *danse macabre*. An
angel of death, in the strange, anachronistic figure of the
fanatic Quaker, Solomon Eagles, prophesies destruction as
he rushes headlong, almost naked, through the town: "This

poor naked Creature cry'd, *O! the Great, and the Dreadful God!*
and said no more, but repeated those Words continually,
with a Voice and Countenance full of horror, a swift Pace,
and no Body cou'd ever find him to stop, or rest, or take any
Sustenance . . ." (21). His almost supernatural pace and apparently perpetual motion prefigure the gyrations of the
plague victims, whose "dreadful Extravagancies" H. F. sums
up with two case histories:

But after I have told you, as I have above, that One Man being tyed
in his Bed, and finding no other Way to deliver himself, set the Bed
on fire with his Candle, which unhappily stood within his reach,
and Burnt himself in his Bed. And how another, by the insuffer-
able Torment he bore, daunced and sung naked in the Streets, not
knowing one Extasie from another, I say, after I have mention'd
these Things, What can be added more? What can be said to
represent the Misery of these Times, more lively to the Reader, or
to give him a more perfect Idea of a complicated Distress?

(176–177)

Between the man tied in a bed (that is shut up in a house
that is shut up in the city) and the man who bursts into the
streets to do his dance of death, limits are charted; but death
is the one way out.

Once, it's true, it seems as if death can be cheated by the
energy of motion. H. F. tells about a man supposed to have
cured himself by breaking out of his house, swimming
across the Thames, running furiously about the streets on
the other side of the river, then swimming back again. The
immense tumbling sentence that describes the episode is
another of Defoe's virtuoso pieces:

I heard of one infected Creature, who running out of his Bed in
his Shirt, in the anguish and agony of his Swellings, of which he
had three upon him, got his Shoes on and went to put on his Coat,
but the Nurse resisting and snatching the Coat from him, he threw

her down, run over her, run down Stairs and into the Street
directly to the *Thames* in his Shirt, the Nurse running after him,
and calling to the Watch to stop him; but the Watchmen frighted
at the Man, and afraid to touch him, let him go on; upon which he
ran down to the Still-yard Stairs, threw away his Shirt, and plung'd
into the *Thames*, and, being a good swimmer, swam quite over the
River; and the Tide being coming in, as they call it, that is running
West-ward, he reached the Land not till he came about the Falcon
Stairs, where landing, and finding no People there, it being in the
Night, he ran about the Streets there, Naked as he was, for a
good while, when it being by that time High-water, he takes the
River again, and swam back to the Still-yard, landed, ran up the
Streets again to his own House, knocking at the Door, went up
the Stairs, and into his Bed again; and that this terrible Experiment
cur'd him of the Plague, that is to say, that the violent Motion of
his Arms and Legs stretch'd the Parts where the Swellings he had
upon him were, that is to say under his Arms and his Groin, and
caused them to ripen and break; and that the cold of the Water
abated the Fever in his Blood.

(162)

"Running," "resisting," "snatching," "he threw her down,"
"run over her," "run down Stairs"—the sentence dashes
along at record speed, spurred on by its verbs of motion;
forms of "to run" occur eight times. It looks like a real
breaking out and a real cure. But H. F., having heard the
episode at second hand, has his doubts about this "extravagant Adventure, which I confess I do not think very
possible . . ." (162). What's more, its circularity and loneliness do not look reassuring. The man has no place to go but
home to bed, by the same path he took in flight, and though
he knocks at his door, no one that we're told of appears to
answer his knocking. After the watchmen take fright and let
him go his frantic way, he seems from then on to be all
alone. He finds nobody on the other side of the river. The
watchmen do not reappear nor the nurse. Granted that

breaking out and curing oneself mean coming to terms with being alone, still the silence is oppressive. Like H. F., we may wonder about a recurrence.

But what about H. F. himself? We can share his skepticism without therefore putting him down as a mere student of the plague. Where many are trapped involuntarily and others by a casual belief that God keeps us in the midst of danger, H. F. has a strong sense of special destiny, a "secret Satisfaction, that I should be kept" (12). Anyone adept at bibliomancy can find, as though by chance, what he wants to; and H. F. confirms his secret satisfaction by happening to stop at the 91st Psalm while turning the pages of his Bible:

I will say of the Lord, He is my refuge, and my fortress, my God, in him will I trust. Surely he shall deliver thee from the snare of the fowler, and from the noisom pestilence . . . . Because thou hast made the Lord which is my refuge, even the most High, thy habitation: There shall no evil befal thee, neither shall any plague come nigh thy dwelling, &c.

(13)

To be sure he is spared, but the moral to his story, if any, is that God sometimes cares for fools and artists. The bodies of other less lucky but not less devout people have filled the burial pits by the thousands.

It is one more version of the artist's privilege, and H. F. comes to question it in the end, finally deciding "*that the best Physick against the Plague is to run away from it*" (197–198). Coming as late as it does, however, this change of heart— which amounts to having second thoughts, as well, about having seen what he has seen and having written it down —has the look of the artist's repenting his art at leisure. It amounts to a renunciation of identity, because H. F. has been a watchman, a looker-on gazing out at the plague from his windows. Like Swift's needy poet, or still more like Swift's turnkey, he prefigures Bentham's inspector or many a Jamesian hero. Imagining him in a chair by his window, we recognize the posture as that of the artist in an age of ennui and anxiety. The anxiety is not only epistemological but moral: What is the artist's right relationship to the events, people, things, in his field of vision that he feels obliged to record? These questions, not consciously present to H. F., define the uncertainties of his behavior during the plague. Though he watches intently, obsessively, from his windows, he suffers from claustrophobia like everybody else and is a not wholly-reformed walker of the streets.

To be sure, watching from windows is not the worst possible fate. Dr. Heath, whose friendly counsel is as terrifying as only good medical advice can be, tells H. F. that he ought to barricade himself totally, never go outside, "keep all our Windows fast, Shutters and Curtains close, and never . . . open them" (77). But even if watching from windows is preferable to total self-enclosure, still it is a sedentary and passive way to live: "Many dismal Spectacles represented themselves in my View, out of my own Windows, and in our own Street, as that particularly from *Harrow-Alley*, of the poor outrageous Creature which danced and sung in his Agony, and many others there were" (177). Whether or not Locke's representative theory of perception is operating here does not matter so much as the effect itself, consistent with Locke's epistemology, of the mind as a recording apparatus, not an agency. We see at a distance the "many dismal Spectacles," and the string of prepositional clauses that follows "represented themselves" puts us, and H. F., at still a greater remove: "in my View," "out of my own Windows," "in our own Street." It is a long way from H. F.'s observing eye to the "poor outrageous Creature" dancing and singing in his torment. Though we see him clearly, it is like seeing him through a telescope. In such removals as this, Defoe displays H. F.'s deprivation.

Seeing H. F. as he sees others through his windows, we feel the strangeness of his occupation:

> I will not say, whether that Clergyman was distracted or not: Or whether he did it in pure Zeal for the poor People who went every Evening thro' the Streets of *White-Chapel*; and with his Hands lifted up, repeated that Part of the *Liturgy* of the Church continually; *Spare us good Lord, spare thy People whom thou hast redeemed with thy most precious Blood*, I say, I cannot speak positively of these Things; because these were only the dismal Objects which represented themselves to me as I look'd thro' my Chamber Windows (for I seldom opened the Casements) while I confin'd my self within Doors, during that most violent rageing of the Pestilence . . . .
>
> (103)

Airlessness, distance, and passivity ("the dismal Objects which represented themselves to me") combine with insecurity, even fear, in the presence of people so remotely understood. What's more, in this case, H. F. shows us the outside world as through a glass darkly. He gestures toward "that Clergyman," but we have a hard time finding out who the clergyman is. At first we assume that it's the "poor People" who "went every Evening thro' the Streets," but that turns out to be wrong. If only we could get out, we feel, things would be clearer. H. F. feels that way, too: at the height of the plague he stays inside "for about a Fortnight, and never stirr'd out: But I cou'd not hold it." The artist-watchman, shut off from the life he records, feels guilty. He sees the people who do get out-of-doors as more dutiful: "Notwithstanding the Danger," some "did not omit publickly to attend the Worship of God, even in the most dangerous Times" (103–104). But it's not clear that H. F. ever went to public worship during the plague: he has his special but fragile conviction that, whatever happens, he will be kept.

Getting out-of-doors also means getting in touch with others: after his fortnight of being shut up, "I could not restrain my self, but I would go to carry a Letter for my Brother to the Post-House . . ." (104). The sudden appearance of letter and post office calls into being a normal world where normal people correspond. H. F. yearns for the normal, as represented by his brother or the Thames waterman who brings provisions to families holed up in ships, all the while living apart from his own infected family:

And here my Heart smote me, suggesting how much better this Poor Man's Foundation was, on which he staid in the Danger, than mine; that he had no where to fly; that he had a Family to bind him to Attendance, which I had not; and mine was meer Presumption, his a true Dependance, and a Courage resting on God: and yet, that he used all possible Caution for his Safety.

(108)

On the one hand, H. F. deliberately shuts himself up and peeps out of windows; on the other, he wanders about recklessly, assuaging old guilts but also creating new ones. In him, Defoe has sketched an outline of the divided artist. At once warden and captive and, figuratively, criminal because his house (as much as the infected houses) is an airless prison, he is also the neurotic escape artist who risks his own life and that of others. The poor waterman, by contrast, lives in the open air and, in his "true Dependance" on the family that "binds" him to attendance, becomes a figure of instinctive freedom.

If it seems far-fetched to think of the shadowy H. F. peeping out his windows as the forerunner of Big Brother, we need only look closer at Bentham's *Panopticon* and its centrally-placed inspector, the family man who shares responsibility for spying on the inmates with his wife and children. Their spying combines passivity and intentionality in the same way as H. F.'s. Sometimes they just happen to see what they do: "Secluded often times, by their situation, from every other object, they will naturally, and in a manner unavoidably give their eyes a direction conformable to that purpose, in every momentary interval of their ordinary occupations." But "in a manner unavoidably" is disingenuous: the warden's task is to watch, and Bentham puts his finger on the covert excitement and pleasure of it. His insight into its entertainment value touches so deep a nerve that it is worth a second look: "It will supply in their instance the place of that great and constant fund of entertainment to the sedentary and vacant in towns, the looking out of the window. The scene, though a confined, would be a very various, and therefore perhaps not altogether an unamusing one."[6] In fact, town life creates these sedentary and vacant lives. The urban character of the entertainment is decisive, the outer cell-block of the Panopticon corresponding to the sprawling but fixed boundaries of the modern unwalled city. In the "Description of the Morning" the sun fails to shine; in the "City Shower" the waters don't reach the sea; in the *Journal of the Plague Year* H. F. passes up the chance of "retiring into the Country" with his brother because, he makes us feel, he cannot do it, no matter how easy it should have been (9).

In all these city pieces, the artist-observer has put in an appearance—as turnkey, as needy poet, as H. F. Being trapped in the city, for the artist, marks his diminished role. No longer the dispenser of order, he is a central stunted figure in an encircling drama: the parody—rather than the

[6]*Panopticon* (see Chap. I, above, note 22), pp. 26, 26–27.

mock-heroic imitation, as in *Tom Jones*—of a god. But, like
the city itself, the artist's condition in the city stands for a
habit of mind that can be found as well in self-consciously
rural scenes. Behind the mixed sunlight and shadow of the
eighteenth-century poetic landscape lay the belief that the
natural world resisted direct participation:

> There have I, pensive, press'd the grassy Bed,
> And, while my bending Arm sustain'd my Head,
> Stray'd my Charm'd Eyes o'er *Towy*'s wand'ring Tide,
> Swift as a Start of Thought, from Wood to Mead,
> Glancing, from dark to bright, from Vale to Hill,
> Till tir'd Reflection had no *Void* to fill.
>
> (Pindaric version, lines 19–24)

These lines from Dyer's *Grongar Hill* echo, however faintly
and perhaps unconsciously, the creation—when the earth
was "without form, and void," and God said, Let there be
light, and then divided light from darkness. But the poet of
Grongar Hill mixes dark and bright promiscuously, the divine respite of the seventh day signifies not completion but
exhaustion, and the void has come to represent ennui.
Creation becomes subjective, self-sustained, and self-repli-
cating as an Epicurean lethargy overtakes the poet: "There
have I, pensive, press'd the grassy Bed, / And, while my
bending Arm sustain'd my Head, / Stray'd my Charm'd
Eyes . . . ." It is as if his eyes were detached, truant, under a
spell and not part of him. Is "stray'd" to be read as a
transitive verb: "I . . . Stray'd my Charm'd Eyes . . ."? Probably: the usage isn't uncommon. At the same time, we
can't help wondering whether verb and subject have been
inverted; does the poet mean, my charmed eyes strayed?
Neither seems just right, and the ambiguity is disjunctive
rather than healing. The gap between the unmoving subject
and "*Towy*'s wand'ring Tide" is as wide as that between

H. F. in his window and those outside. Like H. F., the poet of *Grongar Hill*, statue-like in repose, occupies a fast ground.

But *Grongar Hill*, though representative, is a minor poem. Pope's *Eloisa to Abelard* offers richer fare, charting both the psychological stresses of confinement and the conditions out of which they develop. Against the background of stillness, of "deep solitudes and awful cells," Eloisa acts out her rhapsodic fantasy of masturbation and release—but release into a perfumed, pastel-colored version of heaven that bespeaks nostalgia, if not a kind of decadence. In her solitary dance of death she enacts the same unconscious ritual as the victim of the plague who danced naked in the streets, not knowing one ecstasy from another. She also projects onto the landscape of heaven an exotic version of the pastoral luxuriance supposed to lie just the other side, inaccessibly, of the city or, in this case, the convent walls. And as usual the artist stands by, divided this time into the figures of the quasi-divine but impotent Abelard and the human poet whose presence at the very end sheds an oddly cheerful light, even to the point of absurdity, on the sad proceedings.

If the marmoreal poet of *Grongar Hill* sends his eyes off in search of a remote landscape and then recalls them, as it were, to furnish reflection with the material to fill its own empty spaces, Eloisa makes no sorties but passionately absorbs the external world into the recesses of self:

> In these deep solitudes and awful cells,
> Where heav'nly-pensive, contemplation dwells,
> And ever-musing melancholy reigns;
> What means this tumult in a Vestal's veins?
> Why rove my thoughts beyond this last retreat?
> Why feels my heart its long-forgotten heat?
> Yet, yet I love! —From *Abelard* it came,
> And *Eloisa* yet must kiss the name.
>
> (lines 1–8)

At the start we do not know where we are nor who is speaking (whatever we know from having read the title and the "argument" is still inferential). Someone seems to be pointing the way, showing us these solitudes and cells. The tone is clinical, the speaker perhaps a tour guide: "Where heav'nly-pensive, contemplation dwells, / And ever-musing melancholy reigns." Contemplation and melancholy, pensive and musing in their turn, are scarcely animate. The scene waits to have life breathed into it—life that comes with a sudden rush of vital spirits, "What means this tumult?"—only to be dammed up by the ironic view, as from the outside, "in a Vestal's veins?" For a moment the speaker seems to be a technician again, puzzled by the data: he (it is a masculine presence) is looking for meaning. And when we finally discover where we really are—"Why rove my thoughts beyond this last retreat?"—the effect of inwardness is all the more compelling. Now we know that the tumult of line four has been felt as an actual rush of arterial blood, and that these solitudes and cells constitute, in their deepness, the map of an interior world.

At the same time as the landscape dissolves into an interior scene, we have the sense of being carried away: "Why rove my thoughts beyond this last retreat?" Though in a last retreat, Eloisa's thoughts rove "beyond" it. This illusion of sublimity is restorative—"Why feels my heart its long-forgotten heat?"—but the recovery of love generates the pain of repetition and tense subjectivity: "—From *Abelard* it came, / And *Eloisa* yet must kiss the name." Though "it" is Abelard's letter to a friend that has fallen into Eloisa's hands, "it" is also everything: the tumult in her veins, the long-forgotten heat of her heart. She absorbs the world and Abelard with it:

> Dear fatal name! rest ever unreveal'd,
> Nor pass these lips in holy silence seal'd.
> Hide it, my heart, within that close disguise,
> Where, mix'd with God's, his lov'd Idea lies.
>
> (lines 9–12)

What she has taken in is fatality; and God, like Abelard, is unmanned. In the silent, cloistered spaces of the poem, as in the shut-up houses of London in the plague, a self-enclosing wish to die merges with an impotent desire to break out. The results are frenzy and convulsion. But Eloisa cannot let herself go so openly as the dying man who danced and sang in the streets. She has nothing left but stealth and cunning. Her dance takes place in secret.

It's enough to chart a few points on the curve that leads from solitudes and cells to the tinted landscape of "celestial palms, and ever-blooming flow'rs" (line 318). More and more Eloisa maps the territory of her own consciousness:

> Relentless walls! whose darksom round contains
> Repentant sighs, and voluntary pains:
> Ye rugged rocks! which holy knees have worn;
> Ye grots and caverns shagg'd with horrid thorn!
> Shrines! where their vigils pale-ey'd virgins keep,
> And pitying saints, whose statues learn to weep!
> Tho' cold like you, unmov'd, and silent grown,
> I have not yet forgot my self to stone.
>
> (lines 17–24)

"Contains" (in the first line) plays on containment as any act of holding in and as sexual restraint, continence. Eloisa's sighs and pains do have to be kept in: her sighs are not really of repentance, her voluntary pains come from choosing Abelard before God. But even if it is not what it seems, her self-containment is only one step away from coldness, immobility, and silence. "I have not yet forgot my self to stone" asserts a forward motion to stony self-forgetfulness, no matter how fierce the backward drag of passion. Petrifaction is the obverse of frenzy.

This starkness of feeling is retrospective, coloring Eloisa's past as well as her present. Perhaps God was an illusion:

> In these lone walls (their day's eternal bound)
> These moss-grown domes with spiry turrets crown'd,
> Where awful arches make a noon-day night,
> And the dim windows shed a solemn light;
> Thy eyes diffus'd a reconciling ray,
> And gleams of glory brighten'd all the day.
> But now no face divine contentment wears,
> 'Tis all blank sadness, or continual tears.
>
> (lines 141–148)

"Thy eyes" are Abelard's; but the distinction between God and Abelard has faded into a distinction with hardly a difference. As a result, divinity seems to obliterate itself: "But now no face divine contentment wears, / 'Tis all blank sadness, or continual tears." Should we read the line like this: "But now / no face // divine / content / ment wears"? Or like this: "But now / no face / divine // content / ment wears"? Is it about life within the convent walls or about a divine countenance? If the first reading is more likely, the second is not impossible, not if the eyes are Abelard's. But in either case, a failure of belief cuts across the explicit sense: "But now no face divine." The second line of the couplet is equally resonant: " 'Tis all blank sadness, or continual tears." The tears are Eloisa's, or those of her convent mates, or of weeping statues. " 'Tis all blank sadness" takes in more: the universe is blank. The proposition is not the disjunctive it seems to be. Tears are continual in a blank universe. For all her unremitting obsession with lost gods, Eloisa has to go it alone. It is this perception that brings on her frenzy.

The climax of it is lavish, almost a parody:

> I come, I come! prepare your roseate bow'rs,
> Celestial palms, and ever-blooming flow'rs.
> Thither, where sinners may have rest, I go,
> Where flames refin'd in breasts seraphic glow.
>
> (lines 317–320)

At this fusion of marriage bed and death bed, Abelard presides as priest and once again as lover, but bringing him back to life is a kind of betrayal, Eloisa's assertion of a last-ditch mastery in death:

> See from my cheek the transient roses fly!
> See the last sparkle languish in my eye!
> Till ev'ry motion, pulse, and breath, be o'er;
> And ev'n my *Abelard* be lov'd no more.
>
> (lines 331–334)

Having fulfilled her subterranean hope to forget herself to stone, now she turns the tables on God and Abelard, mingling his destruction with erotic ecstasies that reenact her own:

> Then too, when fate shall thy fair frame destroy,
> (That cause of all my guilt, and all my joy)
> In trance extatic may thy pangs be drown'd,
> Bright clouds descend, and Angels watch thee round,
> From opening skies may streaming glories shine,
> And Saints embrace thee with a love like mine.
>
> (lines 337–342)

In her imagination Eloisa destroys Abelard's fair frame, submitting him to the guardianship of angels watching round and the custodial embrace of saints.

I have been pushing the evidence hard. As the "opening gleams of promis'd heav'n" (line 256) and the "dawning grace . . . opening on my soul" (line 280) become the "streaming glories" of "opening skies," isn't there a signal of real release? I think the opening up of the sky too insistently proclaimed to be convincing. But even in a more sanguine mood, I would want to be cautious:

> And sure if fate some future Bard shall join
> In sad similitude of griefs to mine,
> Condemn'd whole years in absence to deplore,
> And image charms he must behold no more,
> Such if there be, who loves so long, so well;
> Let him our sad, our tender story tell;
> The well-sung woes will sooth my pensive ghost;
> He best can paint 'em, who shall feel 'em most.
>
> (lines 359–366)

This self-reflexive and broadly Horatian ending to an Ovidian narrative not only recalls the apparently casual and externalized view that the poem began with; it also underscores the fact that Eloisa in her cell has been under the poet's sharp eye. In the insouciance of the ending, as though it were all play, the poet's voice takes over again. The last line is pert and almost cheery in its allusive conventionality —and not what we expect after Eloisa's projected death and transfiguration. It approaches Byron's mood as he turns the tables on himself after celebrating the isles of Greece: the celebration has been no more than any modern Greek might have sung, in "tolerable verse" (*Don Juan*, III, lxxxvii). The force of Pope's ending is that tales have to be told and retold; that confinement and release repeat themselves; that we all enact such dramas while we're watching others enact theirs; that, as we enact them, no one else's will seem so vivid or compelling as ours; and that when we do watch others, warden-like, it will be partly at our own cost. *Eloisa to Abelard* not only tells of suffering in an empty universe, it intimates that such tales, like the universe, could become absurd in the long run.

From the interplay between the good and bad consciousness of the age, between happy prisons and fast grounds, we could predict the rough set of conditions that would yield a synthesis. But before moving on to its realization in *A Tale of a Tub* and *The Beggar's Opera*, it will be useful to follow Georges Poulet farther down the path of eighteenth-century thought than we did at the beginning of the chapter: specifically, as far as Kant's early effort (before he gave the question up as hopeless) to find and name the center of an infinite space.[7] For in Kant's philosophical twists and turns is a working model of procedures that ironists like Swift and Gay had turned to account. "It is true"—Kant wrote in 1755—"that in an infinite space *no point, properly speaking, has the right to call itself center.*" But, he goes on to claim, the unequal distribution of masses in infinite space makes it possible, nominally and even more than nominally, to speak of a center: since these masses "had to be accumulated more densely in a certain place, and in a more disseminated way when it receded from this, *such a point merits to be called center . . . .*" And, in a mysterious way, "ends, really, by so becoming . . . ." A center having been located, it imperceptibly takes on generative power, as well as providing the coherence of centrality: where the central mass is formed under gravitational action, "It is at this point that all the rest of elemental matter is linked; consequently, as far as in the *infinite sphere of creation* the development of nature can extend, it makes of this great

[7]Poulet, *Metamorphoses of the Circle*, pp. 63–64.

whole, one system."[8] This struggle to link heterogeneous ideas philosophically together is formally equivalent to, say, Berkeley's informal strategy to preserve the stability of determinate location after an adventure in infinite space. But as the issue becomes formal rather than psychological, pressures mount: states of mind that coexisted without undue strain go uneasily together as discursive propositions. How can you have it both ways?

Kant later decided that you can't—at least not logically —when he proposed the puzzle of infinitude as the first of the antinomies. The best approximation to a solution, perhaps, is an imitation of logic that incorporates the psychological swing, back and forth, from mood to mood, but also asserts and simultaneously denies the logical contradictions. That is how irony works. At the same time, for all its doubleness, verbal irony begins and ends somewhere, superimposing statement upon counterstatement, mood upon mood, but ultimately yielding a result. Which is to say that if it is to acknowledge its own creativity it should begin, like Kant's argument, with the worst case ("It is true that in an infinite space *no point . . . has the right to call itself center*") and end with the best ("It makes of this great whole, one system"). That is what the *Tale* and *The Beggar's Opera* both do. If some kinds of irony, especially Romantic irony, undermine their own foundations, in these two works Swift and Gay announce its re-creative power. Though the settings are urban and enclosed, and events random-seeming, the outcome is healing. Though no point, properly speaking, has the right to call itself center, a center is found. Such

[8]Immanuel Kant, *General History of Nature*, quoted in Poulet, *Metamorphoses of the Circle*, pp. 63–64. (For the German text, see *ibid.*, p. 365, n32.) Kant's *General History of Nature*, written in 1755, was published ten years later.

intuitions as these lie behind Swift's casual-seeming question to Pope, asked with "friend Gay" in mind: "What think you of a Newgate pastoral . . . ?"[9]

What Swift and Gay had most in common was the mixed pain and pleasure both took in pastoral myth. They used its store of image and idea to test their responses to the world, whether of metropolitan London or of the Irish countryside. And when Swift tickled the fancy of his friends with the idea of a Newgate pastoral, he probably had his own example in mind: in the steamy urban setting of the *Tale*, he had already done something near in spirit to what Gay would do in *The Beggar's Opera*. Whether in his Grubstreet garret or behind the bars of Bedlam, the author of the *Tale* seems hopelessly and permanently shut in, as much a captive as Macheath waiting for the executioner. But at the end he wins himself a reprieve even more surprising, because less predictable, than Macheath's. In winning it, we'll see, he wins one for his readers as well.

Since his "Imaginations are hard-mouth'd, and exceedingly disposed to run away with his *Reason*," the author of the *Tale* needs continual supervision. He is watched as closely as the schoolboys or the prisoners of "Description of the Morning": "My Friends will never trust me alone, without a solemn Promise, to vent my Speculations in this, or the like manner, for the universal Benefit of Human kind . . ." (180). We suspect him of being a Bedlamite, perhaps the orator who was once a tailor but now "run mad with Pride" (179). And something is ominous about his friends' never leaving him alone. Without the diversion of his speculations for "the universal Benefit of Human kind," there's no knowing what he might do. The sentence might

[9]Swift to Pope, August 30, 1716, in *The Correspondence of Jonathan Swift*, ed. Harold Williams, 5 vols. (Oxford: Clarendon Press, 1963–1965), II: 215.

have ended earlier than it does, thus: "My Friends will never trust me alone." We begin to feel like ward-attendants.

But as ward-attendants we are little better off than the tale-teller. He tells us to put ourselves in his place, to mimic his "Circumstances and Postures," to share his garret bed where "the shrewdest Pieces of this Treatise, were conceived" (44). And if we do not want to adopt his straitened circumstances and procreative postures, the only alternative seems to be the more elegant but equally cloistered virtue of the truly learned. Unwilling to be counted superficial or ignorant, we become volunteers for the experiment proposed to every Prince in Christendom: that he take seven of his deepest scholars and "shut them up close for *seven* Years, in *seven* Chambers, with a Command to write *seven* ample Commentaries on this comprehensive Discourse." All the commentaries will be "manifestly deduceable from the Text" because the text is that of life in confinement (185).

Under this aspect, the *Tale* begins to look even more like the *Journal of the Plague Year* or *Eloisa to Abelard*, the chronicle of a brooding, solitary, shut-in subjectivity. Its motions, like theirs, are epidemic, violent, revolutionary, masochistic. It goes round and round ("AFTER so wide a Compass as I have wandred" [188]), walls everybody up and sets them (or us), like mechanical men, to dancing. Jack, in particular, bounces blindly off posts, wants to be kicked and whipped, and contributes more than anyone else to the *Tale's* atmosphere of frenzy.[10] But for all its epidemic movement, the *Tale's* strippings and whippings coexist with its ironic benefit, "the sublime and refined Point of Felicity, called, *the Possession of being well deceived*; The Serene Peaceful State of

[10]Cf. John R. Clark, *Form and Frenzy in Swift's Tale of a Tub* (Ithaca, N. Y.: Cornell University Press, 1970).

being a Fool among Knaves" (174). We go back to this
vision of a serene and peaceful state with elation and ex-
pectancy. Has true happiness or false ever been more sen-
suously rendered? Or more lastingly? The refined point of
felicity, just a moment in time, extends backward and forward indefinitely. It scarcely matters that it's a fool's paradise. In fact, looking back, we see that it's only *called* a state
of "being well deceived"; the label is stuck on from the
outside. This parody of the happy prison comes close to
being the real thing.

The *Tale* holds in suspension, then, claustrophobia,
frenzy, and a felicity that is no doubt false but not less
alluring on that account. It is like an emotional balance
sheet, a double-entry account book of our responses in an
open universe. What is most striking, however, is the way
its ironies coexist with anticipatory signals of release as it
moves toward a close. For one thing, the author claims to
have set his readers free, though reluctantly, before it is
over, thereby seeming to spare them the fatality of endings.
Like a magician showing how the trick has been done, he
explains the hold he has had on us. It's not our ears he's
fastened onto—as we're glad to discover, given the association between the superior and inferior regions of the
body (201); it's been our curiosity:

Now, he that will examine Human Nature with Circumspection
enough, may discover several *Handles*, whereof the *Six* Senses
afford one apiece, beside a great Number that are screw'd to the
Passions, and some few riveted to the Intellect. Among these last,
Curiosity is one, and of all others, affords the firmest Grasp: *Curiosity*, that Spur in the side, that Bridle in the Mouth, that Ring in
the Nose, of a lazy, an impatient, and a grunting Reader. By this
Handle it is, that an Author should seize upon his Readers; which
as soon as he hath once compast, all Resistance and struggling are

in vain; and they become his Prisoners as close as he pleases, till
Weariness or Dullness force him to let go his Gripe.

(203)

Our confinement turns out to have been neither the elegant
confinement of the King's scholars nor that of a Grubstreet
writer in his garret. Really we've been locked in the grip of
a maniacal author–keeper–rider–swineherd, quite beyond
resistance or struggle because we didn't know what was
happening to us, lazy, impatient, grunting readers that we
are. Solitary confinement would have been better than this.
But then again it wouldn't, because our descent down the
chain of being from learned reader to jaded reader to swin-
ish reader is a last indignity before being let go:

> AND therefore, I the Author of this miraculous Treatise, having
> hitherto, beyond Expectation, maintained by the aforesaid *Handle*,
> a firm Hold upon my gentle Readers; It is with great Reluctance,
> that I am at length compelled to remit my Grasp; leaving them in
> the Perusal of what remains, to that natural *Oscitancy* inherent in
> the Tribe.

(203)

We return to our natural state as "gentle" readers, well-
behaved and well-bred (though sluggish), freed from our
condition as "gentle" readers tamed by spurs and bridle or a
ring in the nose. We shouldn't be ungrateful, considering
what comes next.

For that is the awkward moment, such as Fielding would
try later to make the best of, when the author fades from
sight. It has been prefigured in the *Tale* by the fearfulness of
the author's friends about leaving him alone. It has also
been prefigured by his triumphant claim in the "Digression
on Madness": "This I take to be a clear Solution of the
Matter." This claim follows an ellipsis of many asterisks,
the missing explanation of how the same vapor can produce

the madness both of Alexander the Great and of Descartes. But, though much is lacking, the beginning remains: "THERE is in Mankind a certain **********," etc. (170). This toys with the meanings of "certain" as both sure and indeterminate. But what is certain to come is emptiness. Clear solutions and dissolutions are the same. In the end, the matter (all matter) is cleared away. That is what happens at the end of the *Tale*, and it is why the author, having set his readers loose, warns them to get out while they can. As he goes on to the "Ceremonial Part of an accomplish'd Writer"—that is to say, of a writer who has finished and needs to be buried as well as one skilled at his craft—he leaves his readers "to condole with each other," but tells them not to grieve too much, "not to proceed so far as to injure their Healths, for an Accident past Remedy" (205). To proceed any farther would be to suffer with the author the accident that seems to be past remedy, the conclusion of any fiction, like that of life, coming to nothing.

Sure enough, now the author fades into ghostliness, a phantom figure disappearing on the horizon of thought, as he tries his last experiment of writing upon nothing. The trouble is that suddenly we have made the mistake, despite his advice, of coming with him all the way. If his pen moves on, "by some called, the Ghost of Wit, delighting to walk after the Death of its Body" (208), we read on, sharing in the ghostly exercise. And we may resent what's happened. Could we really, after all, not have followed him to the end?

Perhaps not, but all's well, even so: "I shall here pause awhile, till I find, by feeling the World's Pulse, and my own, that it will be of absolute Necessity for us both, to resume my Pen" (210). What looked like a final ending, in nothingness, turns out to be only a pause in the systolic and diastolic rhythms of the world. Despite its indwelling subjectivity, unrelinquished even here ("till I find, by feeling the World's Pulse, and my own . . ."), the *Tale* in the long run admits of new beginnings as even a novel like *Tom Jones* cannot; and an immortality quite unlike that of, say, Eloisa's bridal bed. In Pope's poem the scent of roseate bowers perfumes over the smell of decay, loss, and death. In the *Tale* nothing is covered up ("Last Week I saw a Woman *flay'd* . . ." [173]) and the pastoral world is not in sight. But, ending as it does in renewal, it yields a modest joy.

As for Gay's "Newgate pastoral," an opera, as the player reminds the beggar, must end happily even if not in a pastoral sanctuary (59). If the *Tale* shows the world turned

"The Beggar's Opera, Act III, Scene xi" by William Hogarth.
(From the Collection of Mr. and Mrs. Paul Mellon.)

inward and against itself as a metaphorical prison, only then to snatch life and freedom out of annihilation, *The Beggar's Opera* shows the world as a real prison that gathers its players in with a comprehensive embrace, becoming the arena of society itself. In *The Beggar's Opera*, unlike *Moll Flanders* or *Tom Jones* or *Roderick Random*, the prison is stage, not staging-ground.

If a tailor-deity rules the *Tale*, wrapping up the body of the world in gossamer fabrics, in fact wrapping everything up in everything else so that nothing is within and man is just a micro-coat (78), tailor and jailer in *The Beggar's Opera* turn out to be merely the same. When prison is the norm, to be in chains means being in fashion. Lockit cajoles Macheath into buying an especially fine pair of fetters when he arrives at Newgate:

Do but examine them, Sir—Never was better work.—How genteely they are made!—They will sit as easy as a glove, and the nicest man in *England* might not be asham'd to wear them. [*He puts on the chains.*] If I had the best gentleman in the land in my custody I could not equip him more handsomly.

(28)

These words do not parody but imitate what a tailor might say to his client; they are, most of them, the tailor's very words. This sort of homely realism gives *The Beggar's Opera* its distinctive air of conversation heard casually in passing or from behind a door or in the marketplace. The transaction between Newgate and ourselves involves a perfect equipoise.

Though Macheath laments his "woful plight," it is not his being in prison that he laments so much as that, being in prison, he comes squarely up against the way things are and that these are the way he has made them:

To what a woful plight have I brought my self! Here must I (all day
long, 'till I am hang'd) be confin'd to hear the reproaches of a
wench who lays her ruin at my door.

(29)

It even smacks of allegory. Macheath has made love, un-
wisely, to the jailer's daughter, promised her marriage, and
now finds there's no escape: "But here comes *Lucy*, and I
cannot get from her—wou'd I were deaf!" (29). For Macheath, prison is the one place where he can't find solitude and silence; he almost yearns to be hanged because he
has no prospect of discovering tranquility anywhere except
in death. It's not, as in *Tom Jones*, that he's made the inad-
vertent error of making casual love to his mother (everybody does that, and that's why, in the logic of *Tom Jones*,
everything comes out for the best). It's that he's willfully
made the mistake of making apparently serious love to two
women and now has to face a confinement more burden-
some than Tom's. For Macheath, being confined amounts to
the social torture of being at the mercy of others' feelings.

If world and prison merge imperceptibly into a single
ground, to be cast out of prison away from its mock-
decencies may mean, from another angle than Macheath's,
social disgrace. As the jailer's daughter, Lucy uses her ter-
ritorial advantages to threaten Polly, insisting on her matrimonial rights, with expulsion: "If you are determin'd, madam, to raise a disturbance in the prison, I shall be oblig'd to
send for the Turnkey to shew you the door. I am sorry,
madam, you force me to be so ill-bred" (38). This does not
merely make fun of social decencies, social outrages, and
social exiles; it is as if Lucy were threatening Polly with
expulsion from the Garden, in which she has been so ill-
bred as to raise a disturbance. The Newgate of *The Beggar's
Opera*, like the *Tale's* refined point of felicity, solicits desire

and aversion, is a place of sojourn and a permanent lodging.
But it is at the center of things; and breaking out of prison,
as Macheath does, is the crime against nature. Everything,
therefore, from Covent Garden to Greenland and the Indies
has to be brought indoors. Not only does the play effect a
truce between prison and society, it effects another truce
between city and country, ending with a country dance
inside Newgate's walls.

To this truce between pastoral fantasy and urban reality,
the tunes and lyrics are vital. In their anachronistic gaiety
they transform rogues and trulls into gods and goddesses
and also show how ironic artifice can supply, better than
nostalgia can, a perfected world:

> If any wench *Venus*'s girdle wear,
>   Though she be never so ugly,
> Lillies and roses will quickly appear,
>   And her face look wond'rous smuggly.
> Beneath the left ear so fit but a cord,
>   (A rope so charming a Zone is!)
> The youth in his cart hath the air of a lord,
>   And we cry, There dies an *Adonis*!
>
> (4)

Venus' girdle is for show, Adonis is off to the gallows, the
lilies and roses are fake. But Gay's model was a wintry
ballad of Tom Durfey's called "Cold and Raw":

> Cold and Raw the North did Blow,
> Bleak in the Morning early;
> All the Trees were hid in Snow,
> Dagl'd by Winter yearly.[11]

The farmer's daughter with "Rosie Cheeks and bonny
Brow" who brightens up this chilly scene does so less de-

[11]*The Beggar's Opera*, with Commentaries by Louis Kronenberger and
Max Goberman (see Texts Cited), p. xxvi.

cisively than the artificial flowers that bloom, surprising and
springlike, in the dark interior of *The Beggar's Opera*. If the
lyrics are cast in a syntax designed to avert the cavils of the
sour—"If any wench *Venus*'s girdle wear, / Though she be
never so ugly"—that is part of the trick: well-managed
artifice transfigures ugliness.[12]

This transfiguring of ugliness to self-conscious purity is
what the songs do best. Anyone who knows the music
remembers the ornamental care that Macheath lavishes on
some other of the play's roses and lilies:

> If the heart of a man is deprest with cares,
> The mist is dispell'd when a woman appears;
> Like the notes of a fiddle, she sweetly, sweetly
> Raises the spirits, and charms our ears.
>> Roses and lillies her cheeks disclose,
>> But her ripe lips are more sweet than those.
>>> Press her,
>>> Caress her,
>>> With blisses,
>>> Her kisses
> Dissolve us in pleasure, and soft repose.
>
> (22)

And even though his prose gloss puts the matter in balder
terms—"I must have women. There is nothing unbends the
mind like them"—the joke has been partly turned back on
him (22). Self-centered or not, the song is not so cynical as
its model, Durfey's "Would you have a young Virgin, &c":

> Wittily, prettily talk her down,
> Chase her, and praise her, if fair or brown,
> Sooth her,
>> and smooth her,

[12]On Gay's celebration of artifice, see Martin Battestin, "Menalcas'
Song: The Meaning of Art and Artifice in Gay's Poetry," *Journal of English
and Germanic Philology*, 65 (1966): 662–679.

And teaze her,
    and please her,
And touch but her Smicket, and all's your own.[13]

For all his egocentricity, Macheath has laundered the popular tradition.

If the adjustment between pastoral convention and urban reality is once in a while crude and parodic, the vulgarity merely aims to save us from embarrassment. If it weren't for the cautionary realism of fair virginal flowers that rot, stink, and die at Covent Garden, subtlety could be discounted as sentiment. And *The Beggar's Opera*, as Empson was the first to show, is a subtle performance:

[MACHEATH]. Were I laid on *Greenland*'s coast,
        And in my arms embrac'd my lass;
      Warm amidst eternal frost,
        Too soon the half year's night would pass.
POLLY. Were I sold on *Indian* soil,
        Soon as the burning day was clos'd,
      I could mock the sultry toil,
        When on my charmer's breast repos'd.
MACH. And I would love you all the day,
POLLY. Every night would kiss and play,
MACH. If with me you'd fondly stray
POLLY. Over the hills and far away.

                           (17)

In the protective embrace of the conditional, the ugliest of wenches can be fitted up with Venus' girdle; even Macheath can be a faithful lover. But of all the lyrics in the play, this one best displays strategies of adjustment. If I were laid on Greenland's coast, or sold on Indian soil, then I would love you all the day—but perhaps only then. What's more, who wants to be shipwrecked or sold into slavery? Perhaps

---

[13]*The Beggar's Opera*, p. xxxv.

faithfulness is a function of disaster. And would it be fool-
ishly fond of faithful Polly to stray with Macheath over the
hills and far away? The ice and fire of pastoral loves may be
irreconcilable opposites as well as representing psychic
identities. What better than a love duet to chart these interchanges?

What does it add up to? In a sense, like the *Tale*, to
nothing. Gay took his motto for the play from Martial: "Nos
haec novimus esse nihil." We know that these things are as
nothing. It would have been almost as good a motto for the
Tale as the gnostic gobbledygook that Swift found in Ire-
naeus. It would be a good motto for any piece that proceeds
by mutual absorption of opposites. But it is self-contradictory, too, since *The Beggar's Opera* by no means comes to
nothing. Instead it creates a surplus of life out of poverty,
craziness, indeed *ex nihilo*. The beggar brings everything
apparently to naught:

Macheath is to be hang'd; and for the other personages of the
Drama, the Audience must have suppos'd they were all either
hang'd or transported.

(59)

He moves from prospect—"*Macheath* is to be hang'd"—to
retrospect: the audience "must have suppos'd" that everyone else, without exception, was either hanged or transported. It's as if we were already leaving the theatre, having
killed off Peachum, Lockit, and the rest by getting them out
of our heads. But when the player protests, the beggar
offhandedly and magnanimously gives back the lives he has
taken away:

Your objection, Sir, is very just; and is easily remov'd. For you
must allow, that in this kind of Drama, 'tis no matter how absurdly
things are brought about—So—you rabble there—run and cry a

Reprieve—let the prisoner be brought back to his wives in triumph.

(59)

It isn't clear whether this is Macheath's triumph or his wives', or even the rabble's, nor that Macheath (though he whispers eternal love to Polly) has the resources for dealing with his good luck. His wives have been multiplying at an alarming rate. First Polly, then Polly and Lucy, and then four more (with children), whose arrival reconciled him to the speedy execution of justice. For all we know eight others are out of sight, waiting around the next corner. Life sometimes gives more than we had bargained for. The depths of Newgate, like the *Tale*'s womb of mind, breed new life and lives.

The *Tale* and *The Beggar's Opera* present something like a moral: that from the enclosures of mind, world, and body, life emerges; that even if we have to depend on a poor beggarly author or a crazy projector instead of a God, we have gained something as well as lost something in the exchange; and that we might as well make the best of it. Whether we are reassured by the moral or put off, however, it is unstable, depending as it does on a tenuous balance of forces. It is not the basis for programs designed to make converts. For stirrings that would bring programs and panaceas in their wake, we need to look at episodes of flight and violent breaking out. It will be a cautionary look, however. These flights and breakings out have a disturbing way of ending where they began.

IV

"Which Way I Fly . . ."

In 1787 Robert Barker, an Irish-born portrait painter living in Edinburgh, patented a device that he called "La Nature à Coup d'Oeil" or, as it would be known, the panorama. It was designed to represent "an entire view of any country or situation, as it appears to an observer turning quite round." The scene was to be painted on the inside of "a circular building or framing" or on a canvas to be "fixed or suspended" inside it. Light was to come from above, "either by a glazed dome or otherwise," with entrance to the enclosure from below. Nothing would be visible above or below the painting. The illusion was to be complete.[1]

The panorama eventually took the fancy of London, Paris, Berlin. And, in the nineteenth century, "vast domes, grander than those of any modern cinema . . . sprung, mushroom-like, towards the sun in half the towns of Eng-

[1]Barker's patent on his invention, from which this description is taken, is reprinted in Heinz Buddemeier, *Panorama, Diorama, Photographie: Entstehung und Wirkung neuer Medien im 19. Jahrhundert* (Munich: Wilhelm Fink, 1970), pp. 163–164.

land"—as one latter-day enthusiast for the craze says by way of evoking its memory.[2] The idea of it had captivated Joshua Reynolds, supposed to have told Barker that he would gladly leave his bed to see it, should it ever become a reality. (Reynolds reportedly fulfilled his promise and went to see it in dressing-gown and slippers.) It delighted the age as much as Montgolfier's invention did, or as the cinema delights ours, and, like the balloon, it appealed to deep-rooted habits of mind. The inverse of confinement was flight, and it was upward flight toward the realm of God-like vision that Barker ingeniously mimicked. In the panorama, the aspirations of the prospect poem were brought to a kind of technological fruition. From *Coopers Hill* or Milton's high-flying Satan to Barker's "nature at a glance"—or to the famous Colosseum in Regent's Park, constructed in the 1820's, is an unbroken line.

On the one hand, then, there were flights upward. On the other, there were flights across the landscape with their intrinsic likelihood of Gothic chills and spills: Tristram's flight from death, for example; or Caleb Williams' flight from the death-like Falkland; or Vathek's journey to the Halls of Eblis. What all these lateral flights share, and what links them to the upward excursions of the prospect poets or of Satan are the changes they work on the quest motif. As the eighteenth-century prison is to pastoral—that is, a displaced image—so are these flights, vertical or linear, to quest. A study of the sea-change that transformed the quest myth would amount to a cultural history of the age. It would take into account everything from the mock-heroic mode to the "pursuit" of happiness. But it could not help noticing, often, that images of quest and flight mingle, and that flight characteristically turns back on itself like the line drawn out

[2]Desmond Coke, *Confessions of an Incurable Collector* (London: Chapman and Hall, 1928), p. 38.

at length to a circle. This will be the main burden of my argument: in Satan's words, "Which way I fly is Hell" (*Paradise Lost*, IV, 75).

Yet for all Satan's chagrin, still his flight like that of many others restores paradise to the field of vision, reclaiming it from the dungeon of thought. That is Satan's appeal to the Romantic imagination: the main item on the Romantic agenda was to breathe new life into the quest motif. It could not be done by denying the new universe, but only by amending the conditions it imposed; a characteristic strategy of Romanticism was to redraw the circle leading back to self as an upward spiral, whether to a recovered state of childhood awareness or to a new condition of understanding. After a catalog of frustrations, this chapter ends with a look at two *loci classici* in Wordsworth and Coleridge that display the strategy of renewal, and with a still more passing glance at Keats, who held on as best he could to an older topography of value.

It will help keep things in perspective if, before setting about the main business, we recall the sometimes covert, but powerful, desire to get above it all that is at work in the cloistered spaces of Swift's *Tale*. Though we are finally released by death and new birth from the tub that encloses the experience of its tale, it is only after much frustrated effort to defy death and gravity. That is the lure we feel behind Swift's images, frequent here as elsewhere, of height and depth, rise and fall: in the bird-of-paradise passage, in a characteristic phrase of self-congratulation—"I am confident to have included and exhausted all that Human Imagination can *Rise* or *Fall* to" (129)—or in the "Oratorial Machines" (58). The rickety oratorial machines, earthbound parodies of the wish to fly and Swift's most sustained fantasy on the theme, provide a cautionary *gradus ad Parnassum*.

It is "as hard to get quit of *Number*," the tale-teller ex-

"The Colosseum Half Built." From "Five Graphic Illustrations of the Colosseum, Regent's Park," by MacKenzie, Gandy, etc. (Ackermann, June, 1829). (Reproduced from Desmond Coke, *Confessions of an Incurable Collector*, London: Chapman and Hall, 1928.)

plains, "as of *Hell*." Hell is other people; and the "Ambition
to be heard in a Crowd" (55), which brings about so much
pressing, squeezing, thrusting, and climbing, is really a
Gnostic ambition to deny body and wrench oneself somehow off the earth.[3] That is why philosophers have been
famous for "erecting certain *Edifices in the Air*." But all these
edifices, even Socrates', have suffered from "two Inconveniences": the one, a sublime immateriality; the other, a
ridiculous insufficiency of materials:

First, That the Foundations being laid too high, they have been
often out of *Sight*, and ever out of *Hearing*. *Secondly*, That the Materials, being very transitory, have suffer'd much from Inclem-
encies of Air, especially in these North-West Regions.

(56)

A foundation laid too high to be seen or heard from has
nothing material about it, and the two inconveniences
merge as one. It feels as though we were looking back to
Milton or ahead to Piranesi, and Socrates suspended in his
basket looks a little like a god, waiting to come down in
a machine. But to get quit of hell and number, we want
something more prosaic—something attached to earth,
bothersome though that may be.

"THEREFORE," says the tale-teller with his triumphant logic, "there remain but three Methods that I can think on": pulpit, ladder, and stage-itinerant (56). The three machines tease
by their interior relationships—"there being a strict and
perpetual Intercourse between all three" (60). The pulpit, in
shape much like a tub or pillory, and the ladder to the
gallows are complementary images of frustrated flight from
"*Number*." To get above the crowd is (often) to put your
head in a noose, the way up being the way back down. But

[3]On Gnosticism and the *Tale*, see Ronald Paulson, *Theme and Structure in
Swift's Tale of a Tub* (New Haven: Yale University Press, 1960), pp. 87–144.

the stage-itinerant seems a more hopeful case, an image of moderate high-flying without inordinate risk, a "Seminary" for the ladder and pulpit but "erected with much Sagacity" (59). It does not court self-defeat so obviously as the ladder and the pulpit. It is not, like the pulpit, made out of rotten wood, nor so precarious as any ladder. And by its mock-triumphs over Time, it actually defies the fate of gallows or conventicle (59)—to which its role as prep school for the higher learning "determines" its orators:

> UNDER the *Stage-Itinerant* are couched those Productions designed for the Pleasure and Delight of Mortal Man; such as *Six-peny-worth of Wit*, Westminster *Drolleries, Delightful Tales, Compleat Jesters*, and the like; by which the Writers of and for *GRUBSTREET*, have in these latter Ages so nobly triumph'd over *Time*; have clipt his Wings, pared his Nails, filed his Teeth, turn'd back his Hour-Glass, blunted his Scythe, and drawn the Hob-Nails out of his Shoes. It is under this Classis, I have presumed to list my present Treatise . . . .
>
> (63)

Transformed from winged messenger to reaper to a heavy-booted laborer who needs to mend his shoes, time comes to a stop.[4] Therefore the author of the *Tale* need not exchange the open-air freedom of his stage-itinerant for the finality of preacher's tub or gallows. Behind all this foolery lies Swift's faith in *la bagatelle*, in *Delightful Tales* and *Compleat Jesters*, and his conviction that it's best to avoid too-giddy heights.

But the age that ended with Montgolfier's spectacular invention and with Barker's panorama aimed higher. The tale-teller's ladder signifies not only faction but poetry, "because its Orators do *perorare* with a Song" (62). When we think of the poets whose vocation would send them,

---

[4]See W. B. Carnochan, "Notes on Swift's Proverb Lore," *Yearbook of English Studies*, 6 (1976): 65.

Moses-like, seeking the mountaintops, Swift's emblem seems almost a prediction as well as a conventional jibe. If the gods were in retreat, the poets' unspoken motive was to track them as far as they could, keeping their eyes if not their fancy on the earth, combining Lucretian serenity with the Christian God's all-caring and all-seeing eye. But translating these large hopes into rhetorical reality was not easy, as the seminal instance of *Coopers Hill* makes clear. Again Swift's joking in the *Tale* is oddly to the point: fate, he says, turns off the orators of the ladder "before they can reach within many Steps of the Top" (63). We won't need to trace Denham's poem further than the several versions of its opening, for these illustrate exactly the perspectival and (so to speak) gravitational problems of the mode.

The evolution of *Coopers Hill*, as reconstructed by Brendan O Hehir, shows Denham groping his way toward the psychology of release and elation that underlies the enormous vogue of prospect poetry. But from the first, the apotheosis of the all-seeing poet combines with a memorial obligation to the deposed Muses. These are the first lines of the first draft, which O Hehir dates (with a cautionary question mark) from 1641:

> Sure we have Poets that did never dreame
> Uppon Pernassus, nor did tast the Streame
> Of Hellicon, And therefore I suppose
> Those made not Poets, but the Poets those:
> And as Courts make not Kings, but Kings the Court,
> So where the Muses & their Troopes resorte
> Pernassus stands; if I can bee to thee
> A Poet, thou Pernassus art to me . . . .

(i, lines 1–8)[5]

---

[5]The Roman numerals i–iv identify four separate versions of *Coopers Hill*, all of them printed by Brendan O Hehir in *Expans'd Hieroglyphicks* (see

These lines, as it turned out, were almost exactly what Denham wanted: just the right blend of satire and elegy, of poetic hoopla and nostalgia for the loss of Helicon and Parnassus. Despite some tinkering, the spirit of it stays intact through the final version. And, most important, the invocation to Coopers Hill—"if I can be to thee / A Poet, thou *Parnassus* art to me" (iv, lines 7–8)—survives *verbatim* because it does what Denham wanted it to. The poet copes nicely with the loss of Parnassus and Helicon. He becomes a maker with extensive powers: by analogy, as a king to his court or the muses to their magic mountain or the maker of the world to the world he makes—not just in the sense that poets have always made poetic worlds, but as a poet unmaking the physical world and reassigning it to his own royal, though imaginary, domain. O Hehir discovers a reciprocity here between poet and landscape.[6] As I read it, the poet prevails over the natural world.

Denham loses his sure touch, however, in the lines that follow. The problems are of place and perspective:

> Whose topp when I ascend, I seeme more high
> More boundlesse in my Fancy then myne Eye:
> As those who raysed in body or in thought
> Above the Earth or the Ayres middle vault,
> Behould how Windes & Stormes & Meteors growe
> How Clowdes condence to Rayne, congeale to Snowe
> And See the Thunder form'd (before it teare
> The Ayre) Secure from danger & from feare
> So from thy lofty topp my Eye lookes downe
> On Pauls, as men from thence unto the Towne
> My minde uppon the Tumult & the Crowde

Texts Cited): "i" is an unpublished version of 1641 (?); "ii," an unpublished version of early 1642 (?); "iii," the published version of 1642; "iv," the published version of 1655.

[6] O Hehir, *Expans'd Hieroglyphicks*, p. 180.

And Sees it wrapt in a more dusky Cloud
Of busines, then of Smoke, where men like Ants
Preying on others to supply their wants
Yet all in vaine, increasing with their Store
Their vast desires, but make their wants the more.
                                                        (i, lines 9–24)

A technical difficulty in prospect poetry is how to get to
the top of the hill—whether by laborious ascent or by a kind
of levitation—and then, how to present the prospective
view. In these lines, we don't know whether the poet stands
at the foot of the hill, thinking about an ascent and as it were
seeing himself in his mind's eye ("Whose topp when I
ascend, I seeme more high"), or already at the top—in
which case he is oddly distant from and observing of
himself. The simile that follows—"As those who raysed in
body or in thought / Above the Earth or the Ayres middle
vault, / . . . So from thy lofty topp my Eye lookes downe /
On Pauls"—compounds the difficulty. *Who* are raised in
body or thought to behold how winds and storms and
meteors grow? If raised in body, how? If, like the poet, they
have climbed a hill or even a mountain with more pretensions than Coopers Hill, the simile has no force: it likens
someone who climbs a hill to someone who climbs a bigger
one. Nor does the alternative—"raysed . . . in thought"
—improve the case much. Since the poet himself is perhaps raised in thought, though only so high as Coopers Hill,
the problem recurs: why compare flights of thought with
flights of thought? What's more, why set the poet at a
disadvantage to those raised in thought above "the Ayres
middle vault"? In thought, at least, he could rise as high.
What is going on? The answer seems to be that those raised
in body or in thought, for all their apparently mortal origins,
are more like gods than men. They share the secrets of the
universe; their seeing is a kind of privileged knowledge.

Like the Epicurean gods, they are secure from danger and fear. In these confusions lie hidden springs of longing.

This trouble with placement and perspective continues: "So from thy lofty topp my Eye lookes downe / On Pauls." It feels as though the poet were looking up at the top of the hill even as he, or his eye, looks down on St. Paul's—a sight that may or may not have been visible from Coopers Hill in the seventeenth century.[7] These difficulties, like the others, are intrinsic to the genre that *Coopers Hill* in effect began. Prospect poets did not value mountains for their own sublime sake, and an earthbound activity like climbing them could only be an embarrassment. That is why Denham in subsequent versions of *Coopers Hill* dissolves his awkward attachment to earth. The poem becomes by stages a bird's-eye, or better still a god's-eye, view of creation.

In the second draft, which O Hehir assigns (again with a question mark) to early 1642, Denham begins to see the problem and revises the one line that had been most evidently wrong: "So from thy lofty topp my Eye lookes downe / On Pauls" becomes "Soe to this height exalted I looke downe / On Pauls" (ii, lines 17–18). Spiritualization and disembodiment have begun; the poet is exalted: although precisely located on the hilltop, he is borne upward by the force of his own imagination to *this* height. But perhaps this upward movement also makes him feel uneasy after the easy-going, almost prosaic, beginning, "Sure we have Poetts that did never dreame / Vpon Parnassus" (ii, lines 1–2). Perhaps that is why, having said goodbye to the muses, he now welcomes them in by a back door. The tribute to Waller's "Upon his Majesties repairing of Pauls" appears for the first time:

> Soe to this height exalted I looke downe
> On Pauls, as men from thence upon the towne.

[7]*Ibid.*, pp. xxvi–xxvii.

> Pauls' the late theame of such a Muse whose flight
> Hath bravely reacht & soar'd above thy height . . . .
>
> > (ii, lines 17–20)

The project, with Waller's Parnassian help, is getting off the ground.

The upward movement accelerates in the next draft and first published version of the poem (1642):

> > > . . . if I can be to thee
> A Poët, thou *Pernassus* art to mee.
> Nor wonder, if (advantag'd in my flight,
> By taking wing from thy auspicious height)
> Through untrac't waies, and airie paths I flie,
> More boundlesse in my fancie, then my eie.
> Exalted to this height, I first looke downe
> On *Pauls* . . . .
>
> > (iii, lines 7–14)

The ascent of Coopers Hill ("whose topp when I ascend") has disappeared; the hill no longer has to be climbed, but definitely has been climbed. And, with location and perspective firmly established, "seeming" ("I seeme more high / More boundlesse in my Fancy then myne Eye") yields to the reality of imaginative life: boundless in fancy, the poet flies through unfamiliar ways and airy paths. Also gone, or at least relocated, is the simile—"As those who raysed in body or in thought" (i, 11)—its energies assimilated into the poet's own flight. (It reappears not many lines later, in the context of his prospect of London—probably because he hesitates to give up any confirmation, even a dubious one, that he has overcome gravity.) If anything survives of the earthbound mood, it is "Exalted to this height." Denham's high-flying imagination has outdistanced his own revision: the specificity of "this height" exerts a gravitational pull. So there's a last disengagement

still to be made. That happens in the final version, published
in 1655.

This is Denham's last rewriting of these lines:

> Sure there are Poets which did never dream
> Upon *Parnassus*, nor did tast the stream
> Of *Helicon*, we therefore may suppose
> Those made not Poets, but the Poets those,
> And as Courts make not Kings, but Kings the Court,
> So where the Muses & their train resort,
> *Parnassus* stands; if I can be to thee
> A Poet, thou *Parnassus* art to me.
> Nor wonder, if (advantag'd in my flight,
> By taking wing from thy auspicious height)
> Through untrac't ways, and aery paths I fly,
> More boundless in my Fancy than my eie:
> My eye, which swift as thought contracts the space
> That lies between, and first salutes the place
> Crown'd with that sacred pile, so vast, so high,
> That whether 'tis a part of Earth, or sky,
> Uncertain seems, and may be thought a proud
> Aspiring mountain, or descending cloud,
> *Pauls,* the late theme of such a Muse whose flight
> Has bravely reach't and soar'd above thy height.
>
> (iv, lines 1–20)

The revision brings into sharper focus an obscurity that had
entered in the first published version:

> Through untrac't waies, and airie paths I flie,
> More boundlesse in my fancie, then my eie.
> Exalted to this height, I first looke downe
> On *Pauls* . . . .
>
> (iii, lines 11–14)

Was it the poet's fancy or his eye looking down on Paul's?
Or, somehow, both? Maybe "this height" was not the height
of Coopers Hill, but of "untrac't waies, and airie paths"?
The question dissolves with the disappearance, in 1655, of

"Exalted to this height, I first looke downe / On *Pauls*" and the substitution of an eye as swift as thought. Yet if the eye is swift as thought, is it in fact less boundless than fancy—or has it contracted the space between Coopers Hill and the dome of St. Paul's in an act essentially of the imagination? Is it the inner or outer eye that sees? We would only know for sure if we knew whether St. Paul's was visible from Coopers Hill, but we don't.

Whatever the answer, however, gravity has been wholly overcome, and the poet's eye, swift as fancy itself and perhaps as free, roams the vault of air. We float freely, no longer looking down on St. Paul's but on a level with it. And the cathedral changes its aspect, too: perhaps of earth, perhaps of sky, not quite of either. The offending simile of the early drafts, banished to a less conspicuous location in the first published version, here vanishes altogether. Though the combination of eye and fancy defies exact analysis, the poet has found the mode of perception he has been looking for.

But, gravity overcome, other difficulties await as aspirations increase. Prospect poem and panorama yearn toward a state of being wittily imagined by a modern champion of the infinite as the all-seeing ability of a "cosmological octopus" with an infinite number of tentacles, each containing an infinite number of eyes stretching out "into all the nooks and crannies of the universe."[8] Both aim to comprehend the whole, even if the whole is infinite—in despite of Kant, who was to argue that the infinite could be imagined as only the sum of its parts. In the last version of *Coopers Hill*, there is no need to look down on St. Paul's, because the poet's wandering eye can be *everywhere*, can look on St. Paul's from every angle, can see everything. There is neither down nor

[8]Benardete, *Infinity* (see Chap. I, above, note 18), p. 139.

up. That is why the poet suddenly dismisses his wide-ranging fancy in favor of his eye as swift as thought. Anybody can fancy himself anywhere. Only God can *see* all things. If the poet could do that, he would be divine.

But reality has a way of asserting itself. José Benardete, the modern champion of the infinite whom I just called on for help, gives reasons to doubt the possibility of an infinite panorama. One of his reasons will help us understand Denham's problems: "Our vision being perspectival, objects receding from us into the middle and far distance appear to grow smaller and smaller until they are no longer visible at all." In its perspectival triumphs, Barker's invention of the panorama defeated its own etymological pretensions to all-seeingness. Denham, on the contrary, increasingly challenged the realities of perspectival vision in the several versions of *Coopers Hill*. By 1655 St. Paul's, though seen at a distance, is vast and high; in effect the poet has denied perspective. But another difficulty, defined by Benardete, stumped Denham in the long run: "Most objects not being transparent, the presence of any opaque body blocks the further progress of our vision beyond it."[9] Benardete has conjured up his cosmological octopus to see if it can overcome these difficulties; but Denham, having taken wing from Coopers Hill, cannot escape the reality of his starting point. After the view of St. Paul's, he turns to Windsor on the west, then to St. Anne's Hill on the southeast, and finally to the Thames. It is St. Anne's Hill that gives him most trouble: it *blocks* his view, he cannot get around it; it enters his line of vision as a limiting encumbrance.

The transition from Windsor to St. Anne's Hill goes like this in the first published version (unchanged except in accidentals from the earlier drafts):

[9]*Ibid.*

> Here could I fix my wonder, but our eies,
> Nice as our tastes, affect varieties;
> And though one please him most, the hungry guest
> Tasts every dish, and runs through all the feast;
> So having tasted *Windsor*, casting round
> My wandring eye, an emulous Hill doth bound
> My more contracted sight . . . .
>
> (iii, lines 141–147)

In 1655 it goes like this:

> Here should my wonder dwell, & here my praise,
> But my fixt thoughts my wandring eye betrays,
> Viewing a neighbouring hill, whose top of late
> A Chappel crown'd, till in the Common Fate,
> The adjoyning Abby fell: (may no such storm
> Fall on our times, where ruine must reform.)
>
> (iv, lines 111–116)

In some ways this is an improvement, given the poem's gathering aspirations. The unhappy similitude between sight and taste—unhappy because it restricts the range of vision—has gone. The physical act of turning has become less emphatic. The sudden shrinking of the horizon is downplayed: no emulous hill bounds the sight. But still there's no getting around reality. The poet's wandering eye, that speedy messenger of his divinity, turns into a day-tripper in pursuit of the picturesque, viewing a neighboring hill. And as vagrant tourist it betrays fixed thoughts of Windsor Castle less than it betrays its former self. No matter that the poet plays down the sense of being visually hemmed in, that is what the experience amounts to, do what he will. It is a quiet irony that the emulous hill becomes a neighboring hill: another case of making the most of limitation and finding comfort in a kind of defeat. Substantiality, or above all opacity, is fatal to the dream of a true

panorama. The poet comes back to himself, like Socrates
or Judas—"If Socrates leave his house today he will find
the sage seated on his doorsteps. If Judas go forth tonight it
is to Judas his steps will tend"[10]—or even, *mutatis mutandis*,
like Milton's Satan on the mountaintop, where he learns
that his flight from the nether regions has only brought
him back to himself.

The poet of *Coopers Hill* and Milton's Prince of Darkness
both seek divinity, both aspire to move freely through
space, both discover the fact of limitation, and both cherish,
inconsistently, the thought of paradise lost and the security,
of its walled garden. The poet of *Coopers Hill* looks down on
the hugger-mugger of urban life, and the old longing for
rural contentment cuts across his desire for the spaciousness
of divinity: "Oh happiness of sweet retir'd content! / To be
at once secure, and innocent" (iv, lines 37–38). His descent
from the heights to the Thames Valley and to substantiality
has not only its reassuring side but even its utopian side: the
stream that was to run through so much of eighteenth-century poetry—

> Though deep, yet clear, though gentle, yet not dull,
> Strong without rage, without ore-flowing full
> (iv, lines 191–192)

—watered the age's longings for paradise regained. The
prospect poem looks inward as well as outward, backward
as well as forward, knowing that panoramic views end in
self-enclosing circles. Prospect poems manage, without irony, to salvage something of the best of both worlds. Milton's Satan, for all his ironic self-recognition, cannot ever
settle on the earth. That is one reason why he emerges from

---

[10]James Joyce, *Ulysses* (New York: Modern Library, 1934), p. 210. Dedalus is quoting Maeterlinck in this passage.

Paradise Lost as partly a comic figure, an everlasting jumping-jack whose passion for high-flying and grand outlooks produces extravagant outlays of energy:

> One Gate there only was, and that look'd East
> On th' other side: which when th' arch-felon saw
> Due entrance he disdain'd, and in contempt,
> At one slight bound high overleap'd all bound
> Of Hill or highest Wall, and sheer within
> Lights on his feet.
>
> (IV, lines 178-183)

The contempt for due entrance and the mighty bound that overleaps all bound partake of childish self-advertisement as well as of the demonic; for a moment Satan's defiance of gravity is playfully alluring. Who would not like to walk on the moon, bouncing higher and higher? But, having landed on his feet, Satan refuses to stay put. He flies up to the top of the Tree of Life to look about and lay his plans:

> Thence up he flew, and on the Tree of Life,
> The middle Tree and highest there that grew,
> Sat like a Cormorant; yet not true Life
> Thereby regain'd, but sat devising Death
> To them who liv'd; nor on the virtue thought
> Of that life-living Plant, but only us'd
> For prospect, what well us'd had been the pledge
> Of immortality.
>
> (IV, lines 194–201)

Over and over Satan reenacts the drama of rising only to fall. He mimics God's "prospect high" (III, 77), while Milton takes one rhetorical precaution after another to bring him back down. He is a cormorant waiting to dive, a wolf, a toad, a serpent, or even, as he bounds over the walls of paradise, a second-story artist:

> Or as a Thief bent to unhoard the cash
> Of some rich Burgher, whose substantial doors,

> Cross-barr'd and bolted fast, fear no assault,
> In at the window climbs, or o'er the tiles:
> So clomb this first grand Thief into God's Fold.
>   (IV, lines 188–192)

For all his contempt of limits, Satan turns out to be ludicrously earthbound; the verse struggles and lurches, turning almost to prose—"In at the window climbs, or o'er the tiles"—stranding Satan the burglar like a cartoon villain half in and half out of the window, fixed and framed there by the gravitational force of Milton's heavy hand.

From here one might move on to angles of motion more subtle than the ups and downs charted so far: for example, to the flight that Eloisa presses on Abelard, "No, fly me, fly me! far as Pole from Pole; / Rise *Alps* between us! and whole oceans roll!" (lines 289–290)—an imperative that manages to suggest God's retreat to the fastness of space while circumscribing movement by the identity, at either extreme, of the poles; and circumscribing vision by the Alps that separate Abelard from his creation, Eloisa. But, once back on earth, the topography of flight becomes more various in any case without any critical laboring after subtlety. Among the fictions we are coming to, *Tristram Shandy* differs in the simplest fashion from *Caleb Williams* because Tristram escapes (temporarily) the insularity Caleb is condemned to; and *Vathek* differs from both of them by its framing of the Caliph's linear voyage within a pattern of ascent (to Vathek's tower) and descent (to Eblis). What remain constant, however, as we come down out of the clouds, are the self-canceling nature of these flights and their intimations, or more than intimations, of a paradise lost.

The most wonderful of these earthbound flights is Tristram Shandy's. If Toby withdraws into impotence, silence, and the death-laden fantasies of his imagination, Tristram flees death, reaches out and across boundaries, and even

finds a transient paradise in an open plain. Yet he also finds
in flight that death is an inner principle, and his tale ends (in
Volume IX) with Walter Shandy's diatribe against procreation and with the sad case of Walter's bull failing to im-
pregnate Obadiah's cow. It is as if Tristram's father were
putting him to death in the imagination, willing him not to
have been. The fantasy, parallel to that of the very first
chapter in which Tristram ponders the badly-managed
moment of his conception, is one of annihilation, a return to
a state beyond and before the womb. But that is looking
ahead; at moments in Volume VII, which records Tristram's
flight, we feel release, even ecstasy.

Death having knocked on his door as the volume begins, Tristram plans countermeasures: "Had I not better,
Eugenius, fly for my life?" Eugenius agrees, and Tristram's
imagination speeds off. It is going to be quite a chase, maybe
even a dance, in which Tristram with his spider-legs mimics
and leads the figure of Death himself.

> . . . Then by heaven! I will lead him a dance he little thinks of—for
> I will gallop, quoth I, without looking once behind me to the banks
> of the *Garonne*; and if I hear him clattering at my heels—I'll
> scamper away to mount *Vesuvius*—from thence to *Joppa*, and from
> *Joppa* to the world's end, where, if he follows me, I pray God he
> may break his neck—
>
> (480)

With this the narrative leaps into motion, spurred on by
such rhetorical energies that we almost believe in this most
quixotic of projects. We want Tristram to hurry along and
outrun death. And, in a manner of speaking, he does. The
artist defeats death by creating lives that outlast his own.
But cutting across this turn of wit is the counterturn: the
artist, now in the person of Tristram himself, embodies

death, and his characters are stillborn. He leads, rather than follows, the *danse macabre*. The choreography of Volume VII gives to the everyday silliness of the grand tour an overlay of mystery. Sterne reconsecrates the secular, no matter that the secular thrives on acts of self-cancellation.

And, though it is a long way around that Tristram will travel, he makes us feel he has chosen the way he wants to go. This is the whole of Chapter III:

> Iт is a great inconvenience to a man in a haste, that there are three distinct roads between *Calais* and *Paris*, in behalf of which there is so much to be said by the several deputies from the towns, which lie along them, that half a day is easily lost in settling which you'll take.
>
> First, the road by *Lisle* and *Arras*, which is the most about—but most interesting, and instructing.
>
> The second that by *Amiens*, which you may go, if you would see *Chantilly*—
>
> And that by *Beauvais*, which you may go, if you will.
>
> For this reason a great many chuse to go by *Beauvais*.
>
> (482)

Set these roads beside the fatalism of the first chapter of the novel, where Tristram attributes his destiny to the weakness of the animal spirits and figures the course of life as that of the animal spirits forever "treading the same steps over and over again" until at last they make a road so well-worn that even the Devil can't change their path (4–5). Or against Walter Shandy's paralytic inability to choose between enclosing the Oxmoor and sending Bobby off on his travels: an impossible choice between unrelated acts of enclosure or release that only Bobby's death saves him from. Against this background of paralysis, the three roads from Calais to Paris open up a range, though limited, of possibilities, and Tristram's talk of inconvenience is a red herring. We can go the longest way, by Lisle and Arras, which is what the guidebook would like us to do. We "may" go by Amiens, if we want to see Chantilly. Or by Beauvais, "which you may go, if you will." The roads are open, and the energy of Tristram's flight is that of mind released from the hothouse air of Shandy Hall. Tristram goes by way of Amiens; but we feel that had we wanted to, we could have gone by another road.

These are elations of the traveler in flight, but other satisfactions—especially those of discovery and fulfillment—elude Tristram. The great clock at Lyon doesn't work. The tombs of the lovers don't exist. And even trivial goals, established incidentally as a vindication of flight, have a way of disappointing expectations:

> ALL which being considered, and that Death moreover might be much nearer me than I imagined—I wish I was at *Abbeville*, quoth I, were it only to see how they card and spin—so off we set.
>
> *de Montreu à Nampont*—*poste et demi*
> *de Nampont* à *Bernay*—poste
> *de Bernay* à *Nouvion*—poste
> *de Nouvion* à *Abbeville*   poste
> —but the carders and spinners were all gone to bed.
>
> (491)

The frustration is the greater as the goal is casual and evasive. If the lovers' tombs don't exist, at least (we think) the carders and spinners might have waited up. So grand a disappointment of such a petty hope underscores the real destination of this flight: the discovery of self as bound to death.

For just a moment, however, Tristram manages to persuade himself that there may be a way out other than the way home. He wants to die somewhere besides his own house:

I never seriously think upon the mode and manner of this great catastrophe, which generally takes up and torments my thoughts as much as the catastrophe itself, but I constantly draw the curtain across it with this wish, that the Disposer of all things may so order it, that it happen not to me in my own house—but rather in some decent inn—at home, I know it,—the concern of my friends, and the last services of wiping my brows and smoothing my pillow, which the quivering hand of pale affection shall pay me, will so crucify my soul, that I shall die of a distemper which my physician is not aware of . . . .

(492)

That sudden eruption of knowledge—"at home, I know it"—is a great stroke of consciousness in a book that edges toward the proposition that consciousness (not sentiment) saves. Dying at home is dreadful because one can't repay others' solicitude, and solicitude is inadequate anyhow. It is dreadful because it is messy and undignified: "Was I in a condition to stipulate with death, as I am this moment with my apothecary, how and where I will take his glister—I should certainly declare against submitting to it before my friends" (492). But it is worst to die where one began, and also for Tristram inevitable.

This recognition begins now to alter the shape of his precipitous flight, drawing the line of the grand tour out into the full length of a circling home. Sterne's text is the 83rd Psalm:

"Make them like unto a wheel," is a bitter sarcasm, as all the learned know, against the grand tour, and that restless spirit for making it, which David prophetically foresaw would haunt the children of men in the latter days; and therefore, as thinketh the great bishop Hall, 'tis one of the severest imprecations which David ever utter'd against the enemies of the Lord—and, as if he had said, "I wish them no worse luck than always to be rolling about"—So much motion, continues he, (for he was very corpu-

lent)—is so much unquietness; and so much of rest, by the same
analogy, is so much of heaven.

(492–493)

Tristram says he disagrees with Bishop Hall because, "being
very thin," he thinks "that so much of motion, is so much of
life, and so much of joy—and that to stand still, or get on but
slowly, is death and the devil" (493). By disagreeing, he
implicates himself. For one thing he has gotten on very
slowly until Volume VII, continually losing ground to his
own life. It is as if he were admitting to joylessness. For
another, he has said at the end of Volume VI that he is ready
to untangle the line of his own progress and go straight
ahead:

. . . even thus;————————————————————————
which is a line drawn as straight as I could draw it, by a
writing-master's ruler.

(474)

Now, in challenging the bishop, Tristram seems to be wor-
ried that going straight on has in fact set him rolling about.
His straight line threatens him with an ending. A line that
looks like this—

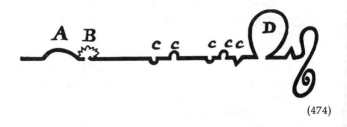

(474)

—has no place to go. But a straight line—as Tristram com-
plains at the end of Volume VI—is too easily confounded

with "the line of GRAVITATION" (475): that is, punningly, with what is serious but also with what brings us, most seriously, back to earth.[11]

Readers have wondered whether *Tristram Shandy* is or isn't finished. The straight line of gravitation implies the end is near—but not without, first, a vision of paradise-regained in a suspended moment of transition. Having "left Death, the lord knows—and He only—how far behind me," so that death is now in fact somewhere ahead of him, Tristram decides to "traverse the rich plains of *Languedoc* . . . as slowly as foot could fall" (534). And with that, as if in a movement that arrests movement, he comes over a rise in the road to see his prospect of paradise:

> There is nothing more pleasing to a traveller—or more terrible to travel-writers, than a large rich plain; especially if it is without great rivers or bridges; and presents nothing to the eye, but one unvaried picture of plenty . . . .
>
> (534–535)

So uniform a prospect frightens travel-writers because it provides them so little employment; having explained that it is delicious or delightful, "they have then a large plain upon their hands, which they know not what to do with—" (535). But this one unvaried picture of plenty, as absolute in its one-ness as Crusoe's footstep (and therefore in another sense "terrible"), is what Tristram has been looking for. Presenting "nothing" to the eye but one-ness, the plain is his heavenly city, peopled with nymphs and swains who sing roundelays and take him for a wandering cavalier. Nannette, the nut-brown maid with the slit in her petticoat, is his Beatrice. The line being drawn by its own length into a

[11]See also Sigurd Burckhardt, "*Tristram Shandy*'s Law of Gravity," *ELH*, 28 (1961): 70–88.

circle implies for just an instant the circle of perfection, not of closure. But it all takes place in anticipation, in the gap between desire and realization: "A transient spark of amity shot across the space betwixt us." And when Tristram asks why he cannot "live and end my days thus . . . and go to heaven with this nut brown maid," the question sets him whirling off again until he finds himself in "*Perdrillo*'s pavillion, where pulling a paper of black lines, that I might go on straight forwards, without digression or parenthesis, in my uncle *Toby*'s amours—/ I begun thus—" (538). Now he's on his way back to where he began.

The start of Volume VIII looks like a reprieve. With some of his old insouciance, Tristram defies "the best cabbage planter that ever existed" to go on planting "in straight lines, and stoical distances" (539). But in fact it is not a very crooked path he takes on his way home: the chronicle of Toby's amours leads directly to Walter Shandy's house where Tristram was born. At the critical moment when Trim tells Toby why the Widow Wadman is so anxious to know about his wound, Toby (ever so gently) lays down his pipe and says: "—Let us go to my brother *Shandy*'s" (643). That is where the book will end—and despite Sterne's anti-gravitational effects, it is an ending of dust and ashes.

Toby enters to find Walter on his verbal rampage against procreation: ". . . and wherefore, when we go about to make and plant a man, do we put out the candle?" Set beside his visceral dislike for the whole business, Walter's managerial proposition that "provision should be made for continuing the race" does not count for much. What's more, we can't help thinking he actually means it when he says that "the act of killing and destroying a man . . . is glorious—." That is why, as Walter points out, we display our weapons, gild, enrich, ornament them, and kill men in daylight (644–645).

The fact that he is telling the plain truth does not make it easier to listen to him; by willing Tristram not to be born, he submits him to the fate he has fled from and (perhaps) thinks himself to have escaped, writing as he still does from the land of chivalry and romance (539). Yet since Tristram tells the story of Walter's life-denying fantasies, it is Tristram who nourishes destruction in himself, the straight line curving now into the circle that encloses nonbeing. We can hardly help feeling cheated as the plains of Provence fade from sight. Walter humiliates us as well as Tristram. And, even though his sadly-ineffective bull is very funny, still this cock-and-bull story bears comparison with another of its kind: "till I find, by feeling the World's Pulse, and my own, that it will be of absolute Necessity for us both, to resume my Pen." The *Tale of a Tub* ends with intimations of birth; *Tristram Shandy*, darkly comic, ends with infertility and denial.

Flying *from* death and *to* it, Tristram as prodigal flies from and at last into the arms of a father who denies him. That is to say, he flies away from and to the past. This emphasizes the ties between *Tristram Shandy* and Gothic tradition, with its ambiguous feelings of attraction and repulsion toward the ages that were called "dark." It also emphasizes the ties between *Tristram Shandy* and a novel like Godwin's *Caleb Williams*, sometimes called Gothic, with its fantasy of an all-embracing but also all-denying and murderous father figure, who represents both the mystery and the social structures of the past. *Caleb Williams* is a next step down the road from *Tristram Shandy*; and, still more sharply than Sterne's comic excursion, displays the radical transformation of quest. Godwin obscurely hoped that this strange book would "constitute an epoch in the mind of the reader," such "that no one, after he has read it, shall ever be exactly the same man that he was before."[12] A paradoxical hope for a book that, in its odd design, denies the possibility of radical self-alteration. Caleb Williams, finding what he wants, flees in horror from it. He desires what is sinister, threatening, murderous, strange, and secret. The projected image of his desire, in the person of Falkland, pursues him to the point of mutual self-annihilation. "I began these memoirs," said Caleb, "with the idea of vindicating my character. I have now no character that I wish to vindicate" (326). The end of the pursuit and the death of Falkland mean the death of Caleb's desire. *Caleb Williams* is a novel of flight away from a goal.

Godwin's description of how he wrote it tells us much about its inner life:

I invented first the third volume of my tale, then the second, and last of all the first. I bent myself to the conception of a series of adventures of flight and pursuit; the fugitive in perpetual apprehension of being overwhelmed with the worst calamities, and the pursuer, by his ingenuity and resources, keeping his victim in a state of the most fearful alarm. This was the project of my third volume.[13]

Having seized on the idea of flight (pursuit seems merely the stimulus to flight), Godwin now has to discover where it began: in contriving his tale, his destination is his starting point. This tracking-down of beginnings leads him back to Falkland's secret murder of Tyrrel and from there to Falkland's character and social position. But character and social position become a function, in the circumstances, of Godwin's groping backward in time: inevitably Falkland turns out to be "tenant of an atmosphere of romance."[14]

[12]*Caleb Williams*, ed. McCracken (see Texts Cited), p. 338.

[13]*Ibid.*, p. 337.

[14]*Ibid.*

Both tenant and master, he embodies the allurements of the past: a destructive force hunting down the present, but a seductive object of desire as well. For all of Caleb's pell-mell flight across the English landscape, a powerful and contrary drag is at work throughout, mysteriously established by events at the start. Beginning at the beginning of this novel means discovering its destination.

Only a few pages into his story, Caleb describes an "extraordinary scene" between him and Falkland. Having decided that no one is in a mysterious "closet or small apartment" off the library, Caleb rationalizes his curiosity as just a desire to put things in order and then opens the door. He hears "a deep groan expressive of intolerable anguish" and then:

> I heard the lid of a trunk hastily shut, and the noise as of fastening a lock. I conceived that Mr. Falkland was there, and was going instantly to retire; but at that moment a voice that seemed supernaturally tremendous exclaimed, Who is there? The voice was Mr. Falkland's. The sound of it thrilled my very vitals.

> (7–8)

We never will learn the contents of this mysterious trunk inside this remote closet, and this has bothered readers of the novel. But is it a failure of control? In fact, our lack of knowledge gives the story its power. What could the trunk contain that would not be an anticlimax? What could reasonably make Falkland respond to Caleb's invasion of his privacy in the supercharged way that he does:

> Villain, cried he, what has brought you here? I hesitated a confused and irresolute answer. Wretch, interrupted Mr. Falkland with uncontrolable impatience, you want to ruin me. You set yourself as a spy upon my actions. But bitterly shall you repent your insolence. Do you think you shall watch my privacies with impunity? I attempted to defend myself. Begone, devil! rejoined he. Quit the room, or I will trample you into atoms. Saying this, he

advanced towards me. But I was already sufficiently terrified, and vanished in a moment. I heard the door shut after me with violence, and thus ended this extraordinary scene.

No matter that a murder is to be revealed. Nothing *in* the trunk could provide an adequate reason for Falkland's ranting and roaring. (Caleb's speculation at the end of the novel, that the trunk contained Falkland's "faithful narrative" [315] of the murder, identifies its contents as the equivalent of Caleb's narrative. What is in the trunk is the tale that it generates.) The "real" reasons for Falkland's behavior have to be looked for elsewhere.

It is not hard to find some, given the trunks and locks and the atmosphere of clandestine sexuality that colors the story from start to finish. Caleb's curiosity is voyeuristic. His ostensible reason for opening the door of the secret apartment—"I . . . intended only to put any thing in order that I might find out of its place" (7)—is compulsive as well as compensatory. And Falkland's outburst gives the game away: "Do you think you shall watch my privacies with impunity?" It is Falkland's privacies, of whatever kind, that Caleb has violated. All true enough. But what would happen if, instead of looking at the book with twentieth-century eyes, we concentrated on the feudal past that is Falkland's natural environment? In that light the sexually mysterious trunk, type of Pandora's box though it is, calls up memories of the Grail or of any object that the hero seeks. It is buried treasure or the girdle of Hippolyta or even Pantagruel's bottle. But instead of bringing renewed life, it brings desolation. If it leaves Caleb finally with no character to vindicate, it brings Falkland to death in life: his appearance, on Caleb's last encounter with him, is that "of a corpse" (318). It is as if a cinematic reel of the Grail romance had been run backward.

We hear about the trunk again later, once more as an emblem of overmastering but empty desire. A fire breaks out, Caleb and others start moving out valuables, and "by some mysterious fatality" he finds himself in the apartment off the library. His eye "suddenly caught by the trunk" (131), he seizes a chisel (conveniently at hand) and turns with "uncontrolable passion" to the "magazine which inclosed all for which my heart panted" (132). But now Falkland turns the tables. He enters, wild and breathless, as Caleb is lifting the lid, puts a gun to Caleb's head, thinks better of it, throws the gun away and orders him to go, all of, which sends Caleb into a frenzy: "How undescribable are the feelings with which I looked back . . . . It was an instantaneous impulse, a short lived and passing alienation of mind; but what must Mr. Falkland think of that alienation?" (132–133). Through the sounds of gnashing teeth and behind the hysterical gestures, we glimpse the true face of things and hear the accents of self-imposed pain. Caleb's invasion of the locked trunk signifies not a short-lived alienation but a permanent mode of feeling, to be represented now in flight and futility. It is no accident that the title of the novel is *Things as They Are*. Things being irreparably how they are, the "Adventures" of the subtitle have an ironic ring. Like Sartre's Roquentin, Caleb discovers that there are no adventures after all. His most extravagant motions come to a sort of hobbling backward. His wild flight of the mind makes him captive. The drama of flight and pursuit that Godwin wanted to write turns out to be a cycle of illusory movement—that is what his design has committed him to.

Falkland's confession that he has murdered Tyrrel and sacrificed the Hawkins family—the confession Caleb has been grasping for—binds Caleb even more tightly into the web of things as they are:

The voice of an irresistible necessity had commanded me to 'sleep no more.' I was tormented with a secret of which I must never disburthen myself; and this consciousness was at my age a source of perpetual melancholy. I had made myself a prisoner, in the most intolerable sense of that term, for years, perhaps for the rest of my life.

(138)

The game of cat-and-mouse that Caleb and Falkland play out after this recognition of irresistible necessity represents externally the facts of Caleb's inner life. And when, at the end, he determines on "voluntary banishment from my native soil" (312), his fantasy of pastoral repose beyond the sea is never to be tested because it would mean leaving behind the terms of his existence. Falkland's agent Gines discovers Caleb waiting to sail for Holland and speaks the part of his *alter ego*: "It is my business," he says, "to see that you do not break out of bounds."

You have led me a very pretty round already; and, out of the love I bear you, you shall lead me as much farther, if you will. But beware the salt seas! They are out of my orders. You are a prisoner at present, and I believe all your life will remain so. Thanks to the milk-and-water softness of your former master! If I had the ordering of these things, it should go with you in another fashion. As long as you think proper, you are a prisoner within the rules; and the rules with which the soft-hearted squire indulges you are all England, Scotland and Wales. But you are not to go out of these climates. The squire is determined you shall never pass the reach of his disposal. He has therefore given orders that, whenever you attempt so to do, you shall be converted from a prisoner at large to a prisoner in good earnest.

(313)

It is a singular speech with its alternations between verbal lashing and milk-and-water softness. Even more singular is "the love I bear you"; what Gines intends as a sarcasm comes across as something more. He participates in the game of love and hatred that Caleb and Falkland play, and like a reflecting mirror shows each one the other as an aspect of self. The very pretty round is another dance of death, but with no gaiety: as *alter ego*, Gines prefigures the *döppelgänger* figures who populate the literature of the next century and their heraldings of death. The terms he spells out for Caleb's existence are explicit and ultimately fatal, rehearsing as they do the terms Caleb himself has already defined: "I had made myself a prisoner, in the most intolerable sense of that term, for years, perhaps for the rest of my life." The limits of the land determine the limits of the round. Gines' oracular "beware the salt seas" denies Caleb rebirth and at the same time confirms his responsibility for things as they are: "As long as you think proper, you are a prisoner within the rules." Perhaps the strangest formulation in Gines' strange speech, this gets to the heart of Caleb's situation. To be a prisoner is to be within the rules. To be a prisoner without the rules would be self-contradictory. If the rules, as Gines construes them, are all England, Scotland, and Wales, then England, Scotland, and Wales are all. Caleb is at a perfect dead-end.

The only way out is a kind of suicide: the murder charge that Caleb brings (for a second time) against Falkland. Having brought the charge, he no sooner sees Falkland, "his limbs destitute of motion, almost of life" (318), than he knows he has sacrificed himself as well. That is the logic of his conviction that he has made a mistake past recall. He thinks of the mistake as not having tried to find some "more magnanimous remedy to the evils under which I groaned" (320). We think of it as a fatal attraction to self-defeating motions. Once Caleb lifted the lid of the mysterious trunk, it was just a matter of time.

Can we imagine any future for Caleb after so massive a self-defeat? It is a job for Kafka of "The Hunger Artist."

With his vulgar curiosity and literary ambitions, Caleb has been all along a precursor of the pent-up artist, with "restless aspirations," "a frighted bird" who beats "in vain against the inclosure of my cage" (256). This image precedes by just a page his turn to authorship, by which he hopes to make a modest living. Coming so soon after his self-portrayal as a bird beating his wings against the cage, this decision is a faint gesture of accommodation, a readiness to submit to circumstance and sing his song anyway. And in the ending, as self-enclosure turns to abnegation and denial, we catch hints of the hunger artist or chameleon poet. If *Caleb Williams* displays with special intensity the metamorphosis of quest, it also touches the complementary theme of the monastic artist who tours his room, who recognizes as others don't that our selves wait at the end of the chase, and who has no character to vindicate. This theme of the artist, though never dominant, provides what sense of forward movement the novel has. It is a counterforce, if not an equal one, to the fierce backward pull of the trunk. Had Godwin published the ending he wrote first, in which Caleb's last imprisonment and madness reiterate the imprisonment and alienation of his mad impulse to look inside the trunk, there would have been no counterforce. The original ending accords better with a static world where things are as they are; the published ending opens a faint vista onto the compensatory world of an art that requires, one way or another, the obliteration of the artist. Caleb, as a man of no character, hunger artist, and chameleon poet, mimics the devotional exercises of the anchorite saints.

Despite Godwin's gloomy Calvinist heritage—a stronger force in *Caleb Williams* than any abstract notions of political justice—some daylight filters into the dark rooms of the novel. For contrast, here is William Beckford's description of the singular house-party at Fonthill that took place at Christmastime, 1781: "Immured we were 'au pied de la lettre' for three days following—doors and windows so strictly closed that neither common day light nor common place visitors could get in or even peep in." It was a "little interior world," Beckford says, "of exclusive happiness," and it furnished the inspiration for *Vathek*. But since what it furnished above all was inspiration for the Halls of Eblis, where the hearts of the damned turn to flame, we should doubt the "exclusive happiness" of this little interior world. Among the "apparently endless passages," the "interminable stair case," and the "vaulted labyrinth" of Fonthill, the sequestered revelers wander in a Piranesi prison-scape; the result, despite a well-orchestrated concerto of sensual delights, is disorientation. Though they denote a comfortable decadence, these "infinitely varied apartments" lodged in Beckford's imagination as an image of infinitude rendered in its most claustrophobic terms.[15] For pure escapism rendered as a headlong rush to self-incarceration, it would be hard to find a better example than *Vathek, an Eastern Romance*, with its adolescent Satanism, its dream of pre-Adamite glory, its tower with 1,500 stairs (it was originally 11,000 stairs)[16], its schoolboy humor, and its considerable power.

The spatial interest of *Vathek* lies in the way Beckford poises the narrative of a linear journey against the caliph's towering ambitions and his precipitous fall. It is as if there were no difference, in fact, between motion along the vertical and horizontal axes. Infinitude renders such distinctions meaningless, and *Vathek* captures more precisely than

[15]*Vathek*, ed. Lonsdale (see Texts Cited), pp. x–xii.

[16]*Ibid.*, p. 171.

any fiction we have looked at so far the feeling, like Alice's, of running fast but staying in the same place: at the place, that is, where vertical and horizontal axes cross.

The view from Vathek's tower is a prospect to end all prospects:

> His pride arrived at its height, when having ascended, for the first time, the fifteen hundred stairs of his tower, he cast his eyes below, and beheld men not larger than pismires; mountains, than shells; and cities, than bee-hives. The idea, which such an elevation inspired of his own grandeur, completely bewildered him: he was almost ready to adore himself . . . .
>
> (4)

The syntax, in its way awkward, has its uses: it tells of inwardness. The tower is a not-so-little interior world: "His pride arrived at its height . . . ." Because the tower is Vathek's pride, to arrive at the height of the tower is, wittily, to arrive at the height of his pride. "The idea, which such an elevation inspired of his own grandeur" is inward-looking in the same way: the elevation is Vathek's sense of his own grandeur, the height of his pride. These are tautologies almost fit for a god, but now Vathek makes the mistake of looking up: ". . . He was almost ready to adore himself; till, lifting his eyes upward, he saw the stars as high above him as they appeared when he stood on the surface of the earth." Having climbed 1,500 or 11,000 stairs to the top of his pride, he finds he hasn't gone anywhere. He has to take compensatory measures, consoling himself "for this intruding and unwelcome perception of his littleness, with the thought of being great in the eyes of others," and flattering himself "that the light of his mind would extend beyond the reach of his sight, and extort from the stars the decrees of his destiny" (4). It is a reworking of Denham's theme—Vathek is more boundless in fancy than in eye—with the literary

history of an age by now to back it up. Vathek's first consolation—that he will be great in the eyes of others because
he has climbed so high—is empty. At best, he will be far
away; at worst, very little in the eyes of the earthbound. The
only thing to do is leave the physical world behind and,
transforming himself into mind, become commensurate
with the universe. He fancies himself a sun ("the light of his
mind") and ruler of the stars ("and extort from the stars the
decrees of his destiny"). The decrees of his destiny reflect
his own light. Vathek stands at the illusory center of the
celestial sphere.

But the way up is, once more, precipitously the way
down. His marvelous adventures across a strange landscape
—"to be accomplished," the stars tell him, "by an extraordinary personage, from a country altogether unknown"
(5)—are all of them a free fall. The appearance of the fearful Giaour, Vathek's tempter and double, at the moment
of Vathek's towering fantasies marks this extraordinary
personage for what he is: the inner force that will bring the
caliph down. Because he refuses to tell the caliph who he is
and where he comes from, Vathek orders him to prison, but
the Giaour is an escape artist: "The rage of Vathek exceeded
all bounds on finding the prison empty; the grates burst
asunder"—it is a delicately wicked parody of the Christian
story—"and his guards lying lifeless around him" (7). As
escape artist, as possessor of secret knowledge, and as the
indispensably ministering angel who cures Vathek's terrible
thirst, the Giaour becomes the attractive force of Vathek's
destiny. He leads, Vathek follows, in another metamorphosis of the *danse macabre*.

Except that in Beckford's dream-imagination, the image
of attractive force lodges in a grotesque schoolboy romp.
Having refused once again to tell the caliph what he wants

to know and, worse yet, having laughed at him, the Giaour gets a kick from the caliph for his pains. Soon everyone joins in the sport: "Every foot was up and aimed at the Indian, and no sooner had any one given him a kick, than he felt himself constrained to reiterate the stroke." The court-iers turn into jerky automata: one kick constrains the kicker to a second kick, and so on. "Being both short and plump," the Giaour enters into the spirit of things, gathers himself into a ball, "and rolled round on all sides, at the blows of his assailants, who pressed after him, wherever he turned, with an eagerness beyond conception." But now the Giaour loses any trace of personality, becoming a self-im-pelled, furiously bouncing, crazily attractive ball:

> The ball indeed, in passing from one apartment to another, drew every person after it that came in its way .... The women of the harem, amazed at the uproar, flew to their blinds to discover the cause; but, no sooner did they catch a glimpse of the ball, than, feeling themselves unable to refrain, they broke from the clutches of their eunuchs, who, to stop their flight, pinched them till they bled; but, in vain: whilst themselves, though trembling with terror at the escape of their charge, were as incapable of resisting the attraction.
>
> (18)

As strange as any passage in fiction, this has stuck in my mind in the twenty years since I read *Vathek* first and is what drew me back to the novel. Private though that quirk of memory may be, it seems worth reporting. But I had for-gotten that the flight leads to a false paradise—the treach-erous valley watered by four fountains of paradise ("not less clear than deep" [13])—with the "immense gulph" in its floor. Because the opposite side of the valley is a steep mountainside, access to paradise is shut off, the sense of forward motion has been a trap, and the only place to go is into the abyss with the Giaour—"The Indian persevered in his onward direction; and . . . glancing from the precipice with the rapidity of lightning, was lost in the gulph below" (20)—or else ignominiously back home. Most go home, but the caliph, who would have followed the Giaour into the gulph if "an invisible agency" (which we feel as the hand of the author, who still has his tale to tell) had not stopped him, remains to keep watch on the edge of the precipice.

What follows, sad to say, is nothing more novel than a pact with the devil. If the caliph will abjure Mahomet, then the Giaour promises to bring him to the palace of subterranean fire, the abode of the pre-Adamite sultans and of the talismans " 'that control the world' " (22). If the plot is tiresome, the vision that generates it has a phantasmagoric strength: "Vathek beheld the earth open; and, at the extremity of a vast black chasm, a portal of ebony, before which stood the Indian, holding in his hand a golden key . . ." (23). Superimposed on one another, black chasm and black door connote the Burkean sublime—images of a darkness that is not so much in Vathek's line of sight as all about him. Little remains but to spin out the thread of his journey in and to darkness.

Finally he and Nouronihar, whom he has stolen away from the epicene boy Gulchenrouz, come to another valley and another mountain, reach a high terraced place, and at last make their way down "a staircase of polished marble, that seemed to approach the abyss" (108). They descend with haughty and determined (surely the pun is intended) steps, congratulating themselves as they go. But pride goes before a fall, and "the only circumstance that perplexed them, was their not arriving at the bottom of the stairs": it is a classic throwaway line, as well as exactly right for the time of Piranesi. Their elegant descent becomes a wild plunge, as if from a height. The rhetoric folds back on itself: "On hastening their descent, with an ardent impetuosity, they felt their steps accelerated to such a degree, that they seemed not walking but falling from a precipice." They are replaying the earlier scene when the Giaour turned himself into that fatally attractive ball: they obey laws of force they cannot understand or control. But at last they come up short: "Their progress, however, was at length impeded, by a vast portal of ebony"—the same one Vathek had seen in the abyss—"which the Caliph, without difficulty, recognized" (108). The long journey has brought him to its beginning. Still Beckford is playing with fake comforts. The periphrastic awkwardness of "Their progress, however, was at length impeded" mockingly underscores our relief at being stopped in midflight. The ebony door is not so much a door, for the time being, as a limit on what would otherwise be limitless. "Better hell than the abyss" is the deep sense here.

But the sense of stability does not last long. Not only do the hearts of the travelers turn to flame in the Halls of Eblis—rather a dashing and romantic fate—but the door opens onto unlimited space: "They went wandering on, from chamber to chamber; hall to hall; and gallery to gallery; all without bounds or limit . . ." (115). This mere wandering from one undifferentiated place to another is the last straw in this parody of quest. And it derives from Beckford's memory of that astonishing house-party: "The intricacy of this vaulted labyrinth occasioned so bewildering an effect that it became impossible for anyone to define—at the moment—where he stood, where he had been, or to whither he was wandering . . . ."[17] Without limit of relation, all existence becomes existence "at the moment." Standing and

[17]*Ibid.*, p. xii.

wandering are one. Like the house-party, the tale is of illusory motion. Somewhere in Beckford's subconscious, the lavish warmth of the house-party had its source in fires of the heart.

At the same time, as we find out at the very end of *Vathek*, there turns out to have been a path off the main road that leads to a version of paradise recovered: while Vathek endures his fate, "the humble, the despised Gulchenrouz passed whole ages in undisturbed tranquillity, and in the pure happiness of childhood" (120). The idyll of Nouronihar and her red-lipped cousin Gulchenrouz, so rudely broken up by the caliph, is still more idyllic now that Nouronihar has gone her way. If experience means coming back to the same weary self, what better strategy than to revive the theology of innocence? But in Beckford's hands, the claim that only little children will enter the kingdom is a counsel of hopelessness. Paradise is patently fanciful when represented as a cul-de-sac off the main road to Eblis. And not only off the main road, but requiring, as a condition of its survival, sacrificial slaughters. Gulchenrouz was a lucky boy, the moral goes, to be rid of the fair but treacherous and sexual Nouronihar. With her, as with anyone except another of his own ambivalent kind, Gulchenrouz would have had nothing to look forward to but growing up. But now that she and the caliph have taken on the burden of experience, Gulchenrouz sports freely in the pure, arrested happiness of childhood.[18] Vathek and Nouronihar have sacrificed themselves, unawares, for him.

[18]Jean Hagstrum comes to the guarded but persuasive conclusion that "pre-Romantic" and "Romantic" sensibility "was largely compounded of a gripping nostalgia for the nest" (" 'Such, Such Were the Joys': The Boyhood of the Man of Feeling," in *Changing Taste in Eighteenth-Century Art and Literature: Papers Read at a Clark Library Seminar, April 17, 1971* [Los Angeles: William Andrews Clark Memorial Library, 1972], p. 61.)

Beckford's imagination—"probing, unstable, but unmis-
takably *avant-garde*"[19]—settles on a static image of paradise
regained in childhood. It was left for Wordsworth to show
childhood as dynamic, not a dead-end off the main road nor
an anachronistic point of return, but a recoverable stage in
the evolution of self; and for poets like Wordsworth and
Coleridge, a principal strategy was to show flight as capable
of a transforming value. The Romantic passion for flight
rests in the context of idea and image that the eighteenth
century had established. And it was the purpose of the new
age to register, if it could, a dialectical advance.

We can see by now how a famous episode such as this
one from Wordsworth's *Prelude* recasts familiar themes and
feelings:

> One summer evening (led by her) I found
> A little boat tied to a willow tree
> Within a rocky cave, its usual home.
> Straight I unloosed her chain, and stepping in
> Pushed from the shore.
>
> (I, lines 357–361)[20]

Despite the appearance of matter-of-fact normalcy—the
boat is in its "usual home"—the mood is taut, a Gothic
undercurrent accompanying the spectral presence of Nature, who has led the poet on. Wordsworth is unrivalled as a
poet of awe; he fuses, in a way that neither Defoe, say, nor
Beckford could manage, ordinary objects with the world of
spirit. Gods have returned, under the maternal guise of

---

[19]*Ibid.*, p. 51.

[20]Passages from *The Prelude* are from the 1850 version. I have compared
the 1850 version with those of 1799 and 1805. The force of the passage, as I
understand it, is constant in the three texts.

Nature. It is no longer, as in *Crusoe*, a question of inert objects, on the one hand, and a footprint from nowhere, on the other. An ordinary object, a boat tied to a tree in a rocky cave, carries the meaning here. An ordinary response—"Straight I unloosed her chain, and stepping in/ Pushed from the shore"—stands for all experience. Otherwise, why should the act set the natural world or the poet's perception of it into such a stir: "nor without the voice / Of mountain-echoes did my boat move on" (I, 362–363)? We know that we will be leaving a usual home behind.

But for what destination? As the circles of water that the oars leave behind merge into the single track of the past, they merge into the track the boy is on, impelling him forward. He finds himself obeying the rhythms of his own movement:

> But now, like one who rows,
> Proud of his skill, to reach a chosen point
> With an unswerving line, I fixed my view
> Upon the summit of a craggy ridge,
> The horizon's utmost boundary; for above
> Was nothing but the stars and the grey sky.
> (I, lines 367–372)

At this point, the boy looks like just another escape artist, flying away to where he began: rowing is an odd activity because it leaves the horizon behind. So it is from the boundary, not to it, that he rows. And the enormous paternal presence that rises before him now figures the experience of being shut off and shut out: beyond what has been the limit of the horizon lies still another limit, the "huge peak, black and huge," that "As if with voluntary power instinct / Upreared its head" (I, lines 378–380). The faster the boy rows, the larger and more threatening the huge peak becomes, until it blots out the stars:

> I struck and struck again,
> And growing still in stature the grim shape
> Towered up between me and the stars, and still,
> For so it seemed, with purpose of its own
> And measured motion like a living thing,
> Strode after me.
>
> (I, lines 380–385)

Nature, having led the boy to the boat, now pursues him. It is flight that sets the forces of pursuit into action. And the boy, like Caleb Williams at the end of his flight from the larger-than-life Falkland, knows there is no way out. He turns the boat around: "And through the silent water stole my way / Back to the covert of the willow tree" (I, lines 386–387).

For all this terror and closed-endedness, however, the boy-poet, now more poet than boy, asserts a new mastery: "There in her mooring-place I left my bark" (I, line 388). The boat has become his. Gaining possession of it means gaining possession of himself, but not—like Crusoe—self-possessively. The urgency beneath the calm surface of the opening has disappeared, as the boy leaves his boat in her mooring-place. Though we can't be sure whether he has tied it to the tree again, restraint has given way in any event to natural feeling. The boat is where it should be, floating in its natural element and in that sense free. The journeys out and back, though they have the look of circularity, represent an upward spiral of the self.

The same is true in the case of another mariner who comes home after a preternaturnal journey on the salt seas and asks: "Is this mine own countree?" ("Ancient Mariner," line 467). It is and isn't. The albatross, at whose first appearance the ice has begun to break up and the south wind to blow, is the patron spirit of change and movement.

Killing the albatross brings dead stillness, and the bird hung around the ancient mariner's neck is emblem as well as punishment. When at last it falls off, "like lead into the sea" (line 291), and the upper air bursts into life, angelic spirits break the silence, and finally the ship makes a sudden bound (line 390) that lifts it into the sky, accompanied like Wordsworth's little boat by strange voices urging speed and more speed, but doubling also as voices of pursuit: " 'Fly, brother, fly! more high, more high! / Or we shall be belated' " (lines 426–427). Belated for what? Unless the ship flies faster and higher, the mariner will be late getting home and late for the wedding. At the same time, he will risk being caught from behind. Waking from his trance, the curse at last expiated, he thinks he is being followed:

> Like one, that on a lonesome road
> Doth walk in fear and dread,
> And having once turned round walks on,
> And turns no more his head;
> Because he knows, a frightful fiend
> Doth close behind him tread.
>
> (lines 446–451)

Once more speed creates its own pursuit. Going home feels like being chased home; joy and fear each makes a part of the spiral return. The wind that comes up "mingled strangely with my fears . . ." but "felt like a welcoming" (lines 458–459). The mariner's ship sails into harbor, and now he asks: "Is this mine own countree?" The prodigal experience changes the nature of home. By such dialectical revisions of the drama of self-enclosure, Coleridge and Wordsworth adjusted the mythology of self to the irresistible motions of the modern world.

Irresistible or not, however, at least one nineteenth-century poet held out rather than adjusted to them; and against

deep-lying inclinations. From the clash between Keats' desire to fly away ("on the viewless wings of Poesy") to the
existential silence of perpetual sound, and his knowledge
that fancy can't cheat as well as it is supposed to, there came
not a spiral recovery of self but the lyrical resolution of "To
Autumn"—

> Where are the songs of Spring? Ay, where are they?
>   Think not of them, thou hast thy music too
>   (lines 23–24)

—with its ending that balances the present against what is
still to come:

>   . . . and now with treble soft
>   The red-breast whistles from a garden-croft;
>   And gathering swallows twitter in the skies.
>   (lines 31–33)

The moment is "now," but the action is purposeful and
continuous as swallows gather in the skies. Like Samuel
Johnson, to whom the next chapter belongs, Keats did what
he could to salvage the values of linear movement toward
completeness.[21]

---

[21]On "the Romantic spiral," see M. H. Abrams, *Natural Supernaturalism:
Tradition and Revolution in Romantic Literature* (New York: Norton, 1971), pp.
183–187.

V

Johnson in Fetters

SAMUEL JOHNSON's life was a long resistance to fantasies of escape. He set himself against the current of the times and that of his own desires. It was as if, Boswell said, his mind were an arena where he fought gladiatorial combats. If he has a modern counterpart it is Ludwig Wittgenstein, who said of Johnson's prayers and meditations that they "impressed me by being *human*."[1] Tormented figures, both of them, Johnson and Wittgenstein both believed that the captivity of common forms, especially linguistic forms, provided a secular analog to the captivity and service that had been perfect freedom.

In September 1777, Johnson and Boswell talked about "employment" as a way of holding off weariness and melancholy. Boswell recounts the conversation in the *Life*.

[1]Norman Malcolm, *Ludwig Wittgenstein: A Memoir* (Oxford: Oxford University Press, 1962), p. 44. The comparison between Johnson and Wittgenstein could be extended considerably further. Compare, for instance, Johnson's remark that we need more to be reminded of old truths than informed of new ones with Wittgenstein's belief that the purpose of philosophy is to assemble reminders.

Teasing Johnson with the mythology of primitivism, Boswell tells him of "an American savage" who had asked a European whether money would "purchase *occupation*?" Johnson catches what is wrong with the story: "Depend upon it, Sir, this saying is too refined for a savage." Where Johnson says "too refined," we would merely say, "That is not how primitive people talk." Whatever the "savage" did or didn't say, some intermediary (possibly Boswell himself) has translated the sentiment into Johnsonian speech. Hearing the story, Johnson would have recognized a version of his own style masquerading as the speech of an American Indian but saying something he would not have said. He takes the challenge: "And, Sir, money *will* purchase occupation; it will purchase all the conveniences of life; it will purchase variety of company; it will purchase all sorts of entertainment" (860).

It is characteristic of Johnson to snatch affirmation out of the jaws of denial. Even at his most flamboyant and contradictory, as in his kicking of the rock to refute Berkeley, he gathers the force of his opponent's position into his own.[2] In this case of the "American savage," what he does is to offer a critique of nostalgic primitivism by taking a hard look at the facts of language. Primitivism will never do for us, he is saying, because the forms of our language are incompatible with it. In a primitive state—to the discovery and consecration of which the age devoted so much intellectual energy—we would not know what to *say*, no matter that we might, like Crusoe, know what to do. What does it mean to ask, in the state of nature, whether money will purchase occupation? The question defies construction because the meanings of "purchase" and "occupation" inti-

[2]See H. F. Hallett, "Dr. Johnson's Refutation of Bishop Berkeley," *Mind*, n.s. 56 (1947): 132–147. Hallett argues that Johnson's refutation of Berkeley, far from being naive or inept, is philosophically sound.

mately depend on the forms of life they are grounded in. A savage would not have our forms of life at his command and still be a savage. He would be instead—as a number of African blacks in fact became—an eighteenth-century Englishman, or a good imitation of one.

Johnson's response—"Sir, money *will* purchase occupation; it will purchase all the conveniences of life; it will purchase variety of company; it will purchase all sorts of entertainment"—brings the question to a definition, filling up the metaphorical vacancy of the original "Will it purchase *occupation*?" with the substantiality of actual life. What is one occupied by if not the conveniences of life, variety of company, and all sorts of entertainment? The abstract and suspended notion of occupation gets a solid weight of reference, even though it is to notions not less general than itself: occupation finds a meaning, that is, by a process of accretion within a context—the process Johnson has in mind, as a prerequisite to understanding, when he says that "this saying is too refined for a savage." Whether we used our language unaltered in a primitive state ("Will it purchase *occupation*?") or tried to use it in a way appropriate to the state of innocence and the green world, we would end up with highly metaphorical speech, pregnant with meanings that turn out to be false because not there at all, a frustrating shell-game with no token beneath any of the shells.

Trying to talk the way inhabitants of the green world would talk if they knew our tongue is the case, Johnson would say, of "pastoral" speech in general, and especially of Milton's *Lycidas*. Johnson's feelings about pastoral language run parallel to his feelings about pastoral fantasies and other dreams of secular release; the one set of doubts underlies and substantiates the other, for in the language of pastoral Johnson discovers the same flight from world and self that

he discovers in the fantasy of escape to America or to
whatever other happy valleys the age thought it had discovered:

> [*Lycidas*] is not to be considered as the effusion of real passion; for
> passion runs not after remote allusions and obscure opinions.
> Passion plucks no berries from the myrtle and ivy, nor calls upon
> Arethuse and Mincius, nor tells of 'rough satyrs and fauns with
> cloven heel.' 'Where there is leisure for fiction there is little grief.'
>   ("Milton," 163)

Where Milton has gone wrong is to run after remote allusions and obscure opinions, supposing that if he and Edward King had lived in the green world, then that is how
they would have talked. But to run after remoteness and
obscurity is to run away from grief and cultivate an almost
Gothic perversity. In the nuances of Johnson's critical vocabulary—"remote," "obscure," "runs not after"—he locates the strong underground current that joins pastoral and
Gothic modes.

In the world of *Lycidas* as in that (say) of *The Castle of
Otranto*, language is on holiday from reference, and anything can happen. That is what bothers Johnson about
these lines:

> We drove afield, and both together heard
> What time the Grey-fly winds her sultry horn,
> Batt'ning our flocks with the fresh dews of night.
>   (*Lycidas*, lines 27–29)

Johnson's comment is nicely and intentionally flatfooted:
"We know that they never drove a field, and that they had
no flocks to batten." He catches Milton's erudition and
iambic subtleties, still to be heard faintly in this comeback,
in the web of everyday speech. It is the same kind of tactic
he had used to deal with Boswell's too-refined savage.
Johnson forces Boswell to think about what he or his savage
is saying; he forces us to find out, if we can, what Milton is

talking about. On reflection it's hard to deny the proposition that we really don't know: "and though it be allowed that the representation may be allegorical, the true meaning is so uncertain and remote that it is never sought because it cannot be known when it is found" ("Milton," 164). The language of *Lycidas* throbs with false meanings. In it, as in the language of Boswell's savage, Johnson discovers still another version of Satan's truth: "Which way I fly." But Johnson deepens the proposition: the flight from self into the green world brings one face to face with the self as it is in flight—that is to say, with a special, intense rendering of the self. Johnson probably would construe Satan's apothegm not as a question of destination—not as meaning that Satan finds himself in hell even in paradise—but as one of process, as meaning that hell exists in the flight from hell, a flight that is in Satan's case a matter of perpetual motion.

As with the escapist language of *Lycidas*, so with any fantasy, such as Cowley's, of actual escape to the green world. Cowley's transatlantic longings stir Johnson to weary amusement:

> The privacy, therefore, of [Cowley's] hermitage might have been safe enough from violation, though he had chosen it within the limits of his native island; he might have found here preservatives against the "vanities" and "vexations" of the world, not less efficacious than those which the woods or fields of America could afford him: but having once his mind imbittered with disgust, he conceived it impossible to be far enough from the cause of his uneasiness; and was posting away with the expedition of a coward, who, for want of venturing to look behind him, thinks the enemy perpetually at his heels.

Rambler 6 (III:34)

The only difference between Cowley's fictions and Milton's in *Lycidas*, in Johnson's view, is that Milton reflects in language the distance that separates him from his subject, while Cowley projects himself into the far-off American landscape in hope of escaping the cause of his uneasiness. Johnson knows how much that landscape, like that of Cowley's native island, is in fact of the mind. That is why he confers on "the privacy . . . of [Cowley's] hermitage" a substantive reality: it is not just that Cowley might have found privacy anywhere he wanted, it is also that the "privacy . . . of his hermitage" is a mental construct, well fabricated, of his own devising. That mental construct dominates the paragraph: everything is subordinate to it, and the simpler formulation that follows—"he might have found here . . ."—does not get us back to the world outside the mind, for "here" is by now within. Indeed, "his native island" carries rich though sad overtones, being another of the islands where the age found itself exiled. Yet there are no limits, Johnson is showing, to Cowley's native island, nor anything tangible. His visions of America, for all its woods and fields, fasten on none of the things that Crusoe had to solace him, nothing substantial such as Gulliver brought home from Brobdingnag and Lilliput, none of Toby's maps or sentry boxes—none of the things, that is, that for better or worse comfort the islander. Cowley's fantasies involve a willful letting go. The limits of his native island yield to the unenclosed woods and fields of America, but both landscapes are the same.

The latent Gothicism of Milton's flight into the pastoral world, as Johnson perceives it, surfaces again as he describes Cowley's case: "Having once his mind imbittered with disgust, he conceived it impossible to be far enough from the cause of his uneasiness; and was posting away with the expedition of a coward, who, for want of venturing to look behind him, thinks the enemy perpetually at his heels." The terror is that we don't know the cause of Cowley's uneasiness. Deep as we are in the mind, it is hard if not impossible to recover any reason for it. Really the reason no longer exists, if it ever did: the cause of the poet's uneasiness is that he is "imbittered with disgust." The mind feeds on its own dis-ease. It is in this light that we have to understand Johnson's prejudice against the American colonies, which was as much psychological as political. It is no wonder, even if some of us find it regrettable, that he thought taxation of a fantastical people who dreamed of paradise regained as no tyranny.

But Cowley and the colonists were relatively easy marks. More subtle strategies than theirs—the self-worshipping habits of prospect-seekers, or nostalgia for the womb—required more subtle analyses and at the same time solicited Johnson more strongly. It is no coincidence that he uses his *alter ego* Imlac for some of his toughest probing; as he does, for example, with Imlac's first venture on the sea. "My heart bounded like that of a prisoner escaped," Imlac says, but his exhilaration does not last long:

WHEN I first entered upon the world of waters, and lost sight of land, I looked round about me with pleasing terrour, and thinking my soul enlarged by the boundless prospect, imagined that I could gaze round for ever without satiety: but, in a short time, I grew weary of looking on barren uniformity, where I could only see again what I had already seen. I then descended into the ship, and doubted for a while whether all my future pleasures would not end like this in disgust and disappointment.

(*Rasselas,* 22, 23)

This is Johnson at his richest and best. The sailing outward into the ocean of space is also a return to maternal waters and the undifferentiated self, a rite of passage ("WHEN I first entered upon the world") to a world of waters, which is therefore not what we would usually call a world: that is, in the definition Johnson borrowed from Locke for the *Dictionary*, a "great collective idea of all bodies whatever." The

uniformity of the ocean clashes with its imputed world-
liness; it is "disembodied." The beginning of the passage
recreates longings that are infinite, unworldly.

What's more, Imlac's view of the ocean mimics, even to
the point of parody, the act of divine perception. When he
enters the world of waters and loses sight of land, he ac-
quires a godlike eye: "I looked round about me." We sense
an echo of divine satisfaction in "pleasing terrour." (Wasn't
God frightened by the infinite spaces of the universe that he
not only made but was coextensive with? Wasn't he scared
of his own vastness?) What Imlac sees, and thinks his soul
enlarged by, is a "boundless prospect." The hyperbole of
"boundless" underscores the apotheosis that prospective
views confer, and what follows has a touch of Crusoe-like
mock dignity, or even Satan-like false dignity: "I . . . imagined that I could gaze round for ever without satiety; but,
in a short time, I grew weary of looking on barren uniformity, where I could only see again what I had already
seen." The human reality of "in a short time" balances
the fiction of divine timelessness; Imlac imagines that
he could gaze round "for ever," as God does, only to discover that he grows weary of sameness. The God who sees
all things at all times in all places can only see again what he
has already seen. Aspiring to be God, from the angle of
actual human vision, is aspiring to infinite sameness and
tedium: in the eye of God, does ripe fruit never fall? Or,
rather, is it always falling though always on the tree? The
ocean, comparable to Tristram's "unvaried picture of plenty," gives the travel-writer nothing to write about.

Having learned this much, Imlac goes below: "I then
descended into the ship, and doubted for a while whether
all my future pleasures would not end like this in disgust
and disappointment." The pattern of movement across the

landscape, dominant at the start of the passage but then changed, potentially, by the boundless "prospect," now changes in fact to that of ascent and descent. The drama of flight away from, such as Cowley's imaginary flight to America, is the same drama on a different axis as that of flight upward toward the divine, and Imlac fears he may have to repeat it over and over. Glancing at the temporal meaning of "prospect" as "a view into futurity," he wonders whether all his future pleasures will not end in disgust and disappointment. We remember Cowley, embittered with disgust, and the repetitive circularity of his fantasies. What ends in disgust lures the mind into repeated flights from the cause of its uneasiness, therefore repeated prospects, repeatedly pleasing terrors, and repeated weariness with the sameness of it—which is also to say, with the sameness of the pattern endlessly traced out.

But Imlac, being Johnson's *alter ego*, prescribes the Johnsonian antidote:

Yet, surely, said I, the ocean and the land are very different; the only variety of water is rest and motion, but the earth has mountains and vallies, desarts and cities: it is inhabited by men of different customs and contrary opinions; and I may hope to find variety in life, though I should miss it in nature.

(23–24)

By variety or "novelty," as Johnson sometimes calls it, the mind breaks out of its self-enclosing patterns.[3] The movement has shifted again, this time off the vertical axis: *ocean* and *land* now stand respectively for the flight *away from* and the flight *back to* reality. Ocean equals *nature*, which equals in this case a kind of death wish: rest prevails over, because it

[3]On the psychological uses of variety in Johnson, see Walter Jackson Bate, *The Achievement of Samuel Johnson* (New York: Oxford University Press, 1955), esp. pp. 65–72.

is prior to, motion. Land or earth equals *life*. The mountains of earth are not images of divine aspiration, but part of the variety of earth, which includes deserts and cities and men of different customs and contrary opinions. In the Johnsonian standard of variety, the old values of an ordered and harmonious universe find new expression. That old order, newly constituted, Johnson identifies with life itself. We can better understand his hesitant response to the natural world in the face of Imlac's juxtaposition: "I may hope to find variety in life, though I should miss it in nature." Nature is defined here as what is not life; the usage is not uncommon, but it is telling. Life can't help but include the life of the perceiver. Johnson affirms the radical value not only of life, but of living.

Of living, and therefore also of knowing. Johnson makes the best of Locke's alarming theories of knowledge, even of their materialist overtones. This is from the conclusion of *Rambler* 124, on the "arts of spending time":

To be born in ignorance with a capacity of knowledge, and to be placed in the midst of a world filled with variety, perpetually pressing upon the senses and irritating curiosity, is surely a sufficient security against the languishment of inattention.

(IV:299)

An ellipsis will show part of what is happening: "To be born . . . is surely a sufficient security against the languishment of inattention." Being born, as in *Tristram Shandy*, is the main event in the plot of life, and to be born with a mind uninscribed by experience into a world that presses on the senses and irritates the curiosity constitutes a blessing: the world keeps us busy, as it would not if we were not born in ignorance. The new prison of mind, Johnson is saying, is not a prison; or if it is, we should make the most of its security. Not to be in it would be like being God, and we should not wish for that. The golden age of innate knowledge would have been a less vital experience, in human terms, than Johnson thought life actually to be.

Over and again, Johnson's writing takes its strength from these adjustments between down-to-earthness and the luxuriance of his own imagination. This is what gives such an emotional charge, for example, to the episode in *Rasselas* of the man who builds a pair of wings and tries to fly. Johnson was dubiously fascinated, from first to last, with the possibility of human flight: the philosopher-sage who wrote the "dissertation on the art of flying" is recognizably the same man who, a few weeks before his death, told Edmund Hector a little wistfully, but boyishly, that he had sent his servant Francis "to see the Ballon fly" because he was not in good health and could not go himself.[4] And, fantastical as the flying man in *Rasselas* may be, he anticipates Montgolfier; his fantasies are of something more like balloon flight than bird flight, a suspended and hovering motion:

You, Sir, whose curiosity is so extensive, will easily conceive with what pleasure a philosopher, furnished with wings, and hovering in the sky, would see the earth, and all its inhabitants, rolling beneath him, and presenting to him successively, by its diurnal motion, all the countries within the same parallel. How must it amuse the pendent spectator to see the moving scene of land and ocean, cities and desarts!

(16)

[4]Johnson to Hector, November 17, 1784, in *The Letters of Samuel Johnson*, ed. R. W. Chapman, 3 vols. (Oxford: Clarendon Press, 1952), III: 248–249. Johnson's doubtfulness about the value of balloons had to do with the difficulty of controlling their movement and the fact that they didn't fly high enough to add to the store of knowledge: "The vehicles can serve no use, till we can guide them, and they can gratify no curiosity till we mount with them to greater heights than we can reach without, till we rise above the tops of the highest mountains, which we have yet not done" (Johnson to Richard Brocklesby, October 6, 1784, *Letters*, III: 232).

"Le soleil apparait comme une hostie immense posée sur des couches de neige."

"Halo lunaire observé par M. Flammarion. (Nuit du 14–15 juillet 1867.)"

"Le silence absolu règne ici dans sa morne majesté."

(Reproduced from J. Glaisher, C. Flammarion, W. de Fonvielle, and G. Tissandier, *Voyages aériens*, ill. by E. Cicéri, A. Marie, and A. Tissandier, Paris: Hachette, 1870.)

What Johnson catches is Epicurean remoteness. Here are the same land and ocean, the same cities and deserts, that only a few pages later define the variety of the world—but all at a distance. What is missing are the customs and contrary opinions of men, for men seen at a distance are no more than earth's inhabitants; and the security gained—"To survey with equal security the marts of trade, and the fields of battle; mountains infested by barbarians, and fruitful regions gladdened by plenty . . ." (16)—is that of a distant god for whose pleasure the moving earth, its countries and inhabitants, all pass in review.

Yet the winged philosopher, it turns out, is just another scared mortal in disguise: "I shall begin my task to morrow, and in a year expect to tower into the air beyond the malice or pursuit of man" (17). The fantasy, being one of escape, involves a running away, like Milton's chasing after remote allusions or Cowley's thinking an enemy hard on his heels and not venturing to look back. And, being a fantasy of permanent ascent, it resembles Imlac's passing illusion that he can gaze at the ocean forever. The airborne imagination takes no heed of gravity; the man with wings strapped on fancies himself a bird, not born for death. What he calls "the malice or pursuit of man" he feels as the malice or pursuit of another species; he is Dedalus, escaping the nets of his countrymen. But Rasselas (more explicit than Joyce) warns that many an aspiring Dedalus turns out to be an Icarus at last:

I am afraid that no man will be able to breathe in these regions of speculation and tranquility. I have been told, that respiration is difficult upon lofty mountains, yet from these precipices, though so high as to produce great tenuity of the air, it is very easy to fall: therefore I suspect, that from any height, where life can be supported, there may be danger of too quick descent.

(16–17).

This is tongue-in-cheek, witty, and allegorically teasing. What follows, at least the half of it, is Johnsonian farce:

In a year the wings were finished, and, on a morning appointed, the maker appeared furnished for flight on a little promontory: he waved his pinions a while to gather air, then leaped from his stand, and in an instant dropped into the lake. His wings, which were of no use in the air, sustained him in the water, and the prince drew him to land, half dead with terrour and vexation.

(18)

For just a moment the man is transfigured: did any man ever have pinions before? But the moment is short-lived, a sort of optical illusion, and truth will out: if God had intended man to fly, he'd have given him wings. The land, where Rasselas drags the wet and crestfallen birdman, is where we belong.

Land is also where the learned and dotty astronomer belongs. His story comes a few chapters before the end, structurally parallel to the story of the man who hoped to fly, a few chapters after the beginning. The birdman has shown Rasselas, "impatient as an eagle in a grate" (13), some hopes that, however futile, nonetheless relieve the dead-level monotony of the Happy Valley. His craziness prods Rasselas and Imlac into finding a more circumspect way out. The astronomer's craziness gives the travelers an occasion to show what they have learned before going back to Abyssinia. Not only do they bring him down out of the clouds, they are ready to give up their own dreams of flight and, by curing another, they display their own cure. Again the treatment for stasis and fixed vision is variety of impression. Imlac tells of visiting the astronomer:

Men of various ideas and fluent conversation are commonly welcome to those whose thoughts have been long fixed upon a single point, and who find the images of other things stealing away. I delighted him with my remarks, he smiled at the narrative of my travels, and was glad to forget the constellations, and descend for a moment into the lower world.

(107)

The astronomer, his mind fixed on a single point, sees as if with peripheral vision the other images of life stealing away: these are the Gothic side-effects of monomania, to be cured by coming down to the lower world and its variousness.

Ambiguous though the conclusion of *Rasselas* may be, its strength of feeling is not in doubt: "They deliberated a while what was to be done, and resolved, when the inundation should cease, to return to Abissinia" (134). *Deliberate* and *resolve* are verbs of weight and value in Johnson's lexicon, and the return to Abyssinia, when the waters of the

Nile recede and the land is reclaimed, means going back to life on land. It is not exactly a joyful return nor necessarily a permanent one. But neither is it loaded with the ironies of Imlac's original hopes for life in the Happy Valley—"I resigned myself with joy to perpetual confinement" (35); and in the long run, the irony of Imlac's hopes turns out to have, in Johnson's understanding of it, more than a little underlying truth. Out of Johnson's characteristic resignation, neither despairing nor apathetic, to the necessary confinements of our lives, there comes on some other occasions, if not quite in *Rasselas*, a strange joy.

That, I believe, is what happens in *The Vanity of Human Wishes*. The startling thing about that compelling poem is not only its inwardness but the way its inwardness becomes a basis of comfort. Johnson does not claim that mind can make a heaven in hell's despite, but that it can make of radical limitation a comparative blessing. *The Vanity of Human Wishes* is in its way highly subjective, a mental landscape intensely rendered. Within it, Johnson ferrets out the impulses to grand prospective views and subjects them to a critical reading. He concedes from the start that mind is locked in and that being locked in is what inspires the poet to airy flights and panoramic views; then he argues the futility of these compensatory movements. *The Vanity of Human Wishes*, like so much of his work, takes strength from being deeply rooted in the cultural soil of the time.

If we set the beginning of the poem beside some characteristic lines near the start of *Grongar Hill* (in its octosyllabic version), we can see better what Johnson is doing, especially in his much-abused opening couplet. Dyer's octosyllabics are more than faintly frivolous; and his weather (here if not always elsewhere), sunny and serene:

> Now, I gain the Mountain's Brow,
> What a Landskip lies below!
> No Clouds, no Vapours intervene,
> But the gay, the open Scene
> Does the Face of Nature show,
> In all the Hues of Heaven's Bow!
> And, swelling to embrace the Light,
> Spreads around beyond the Sight.
>
> (lines 41–48)

Johnson's heavier weather—the clouds and mists that seem almost an answer to Dyer—marks the limitations of human perception:

> Let observation with extensive view,
> Survey mankind, from China to Peru;
> Remark each anxious toil, each eager strife,
> And watch the busy scenes of crouded life;
> Then say how hope and fear, desire and hate,
> O'erspread with snares the clouded maze of fate,
> Where wav'ring man, betray'd by vent'rous pride,
> To tread the dreary paths without a guide,
> As treach'rous phantoms in the mist delude,
> Shuns fancied ills, or chases airy good . . . .
>
> (1–10)

Does it follow, because nothing could be further from Dyer's limp acceptance of the landscape, that Johnson's active searching and energetic seeing is the right way to go about it? I think the answer is only a qualified yes; passivity was alien to him (in this respect he should have disagreed with the new way of ideas), but clouds and vapors and mist do obscure the vision, and the human act of seeing is impure. We should not expect too much.

There is no getting around the complaint that the opening couplet is tautology heaped on tautology and that Johnson might as well have said "Let observation with extensive

observation observe mankind from China to Peru." But
what if that were the point? What if the grandiloquence
were meant subversively? The first word of the poem hovers
ambiguously between the casual and the grand, between its
permissive and imperative senses, anticipating either a cool
supposition or a godlike injunction. We wonder if we're
right in hearing overtones of the creation: Let there be light,
let there be a firmament, let it divide the waters. If so, the
moral may be that much more pointed. If the God of
Genesis brings order out of chaos—the wonder being that
he has made something out of nothing—this grand survey
of the world from China to Peru, or even to the Antipodes,
is one more self-enclosing journey, its energy that of a mind
at bay.

In this reading, the tautologies have a job to do, not as
signs of extensive vision but of the mind's banging up
against limits. If Johnson's prospect is more exhilarating at
first, because more active, than the prospect from Grongar
Hill, still we sense that the exhilaration, like Imlac's on
seeing the ocean, may turn to disgust or disappointment.
That is what happens. Not only is the panoramic view soon
clouded over, but the perceiving eye itself contributes most
to the increasing obscurity of the scene:

> Then say how hope and fear, desire and hate,
> O'erspread with snares the clouded maze of fate,
> Where wav'ring man, betray'd by vent'rous pride,
> To tread the dreary paths without a guide,
> As treach'rous phantoms in the mist delude,
> Shuns fancied ills, or chases airy good . . . .
>
> (lines 5–10)

So much not only for sunshiny moods but for the ambiguous grandeur of "Let observation with extensive view."
Here is a new sort of imperative, and here are personified

powers unlike the Olympian figure of observation in the first line. To be sure, the syntax of the first five couplets goes like this: Let observation survey mankind, remark each eager toil, watch the busy scenes of life, and then say "how hope and fear, desire and hate, / O'erspread with snares the clouded maze of fate." But the verbal descent from the em-pyrean—from *survey* to *remark* to *watch* and finally to the unpretentious *say*—results in the gradual obliteration or at least obscuring of "observation." It's not strictly in character for observation to say anything: there is a mixing of alle-gorical modes, of seeing and saying. After an opening on uncomfortably high ground, we've come back down. The result is that "Then say how hope and fear . . ." seems as much an imperative for us to act on as for observation. We are finding our place in the poem, not on the mountaintop but on the ground, in the clouded maze of fate.

The hopes and fears that in a sense, remote by now, are objects of observation are more important as active sub-jects—forces that make the poem go and motions of our minds in a way that observation is not. After all, if obser-vation surveys the world from a mountaintop, and if the maze of fate is clouded over, it would be hard to see the snares laid by hope and fear. The limitations of mind, felt so strongly in the tautologies of the first couplet, now cluster in the image of man in a maze, frightened and misled by spectral shapes. Perhaps the promise of a bird's-eye view was only an emblem of the mind in search of airy good. The pattern of rise and fall, pervasive in the rest of the poem, gets not only its start but its sanction in these opening lines: the pattern recreates, over and over, the mind's hopes for an extensive view and its irreducible restrictions. Some-times our vantage seems to be from below, sometimes from above, but after the panoramic opening we mostly participate in the upward and downward motions of Johnson's characters as, rocket-like, they mount and shine, evaporate and fall. The moral of the poem, or one of them, is that so distant and extensive a view as that proclaimed at the start is beyond our power.

That being so, "Where then shall Hope and Fear their objects find" (line 343)? Where shall the motives of the mind find equivalents to the objects of observation? Johnson's answer is something more than Christian optimism or Stoic resignation:

> Enquirer, cease, petitions yet remain,
> Which heav'n may hear, nor deem religion vain.
> Still raise for good the supplicating voice,
> But leave to heav'n the measure and the choice,
> Safe in his pow'r, whose eyes discern afar
> The secret ambush of a specious pray'r.
> Implore his aid, in his decisions rest,
> Secure whate'er he gives, he gives the best.
>
> (lines 349–356)

It is the service of the Lord as perfect freedom recreated in a hierarchy of perception: God's omniscience absorbs transient prospective views. The divine mind gathers in the human mind, though at a great distance: "whose eyes discern afar / The secret ambush of a specious pray'r." To be safe in his power who sees all from afar is to be secure in his sight. We are seen by God, but "safe in his pow'r" we therefore see in him, too. Johnson's language—like Malebranche's theory of seeing all things in God—aims to reconcile the finitude of human perception with the infinite perceptions of a God who, in Johnson's theology, retains most of the attributes the age had divested him of. We are rescued from our own secret ambushes and haphazard flights, and the result is almost elation, a strange joy.[5]

[5]In the *Dictionary*, Johnson gives only this definition of "elation": "Haughtiness proceeding from success; pride of prosperity." But the *New*

To be safe in God's power means being able to direct the impulse to flight into self-corrective movements:

> Yet when the sense of sacred presence fires,
> And strong devotion to the skies aspires,
> Pour forth thy fervours for a healthful mind,
> Obedient passions, and a will resign'd.
>
> (lines 357–360)

The impulse to scale the heights of devotion flattens out in obedience and acceptance; the fires and fervors of mind become self-purifying. Movement occurs because limits are recognized, infinitude being conceded to God. When limits are denied and human vision is supposed to reach from China to Peru, movement effectively stops. Yet there's no denying God's remoteness and the sense we're left with of being, for better or worse, alone in his sight. It is not an impossible stretch from *The Vanity of Human Wishes* to a celebration of the mind as its own world and its own self-consecrated place.[6]

Nor is it far from Johnson's fine ode "On the Death of Dr. Robert Levet" to a modern celebration, or anti-celebration (Beckett's or whoever else's), of life in the mines:

> Condemn'd to hope's delusive mine,
> As on we toil from day to day,

English Dictionary cites *Rambler* 184 ("Their time is past between elation and despondency") as the first instance of "elation" as meaning, in a neutral or good sense, "elevation of spirits." On the relationship between elation and claustrophobia; see Bertram D. Lewin, *The Psychoanalysis of Elation* (New York: Norton, 1950), pp. 107–110; cited in Brombert, "The Happy Prison: A Recurring Romantic Metaphor" (see Chap. I, above, note 2) p. 64.

[6]On *The Vanity of Human Wishes*, see D. V. Boyd, "Vanity and Vacuity: A Reading of Johnson's Verse Satires," *ELH*, 39 (1972): 387–403. Boyd describes the opening of the poem as "empirical" and what follows as·the "subversion of the empirical process"; the poem demonstrates the "bankruptcy" of the appeal to observation (pp. 397, 403).

> By sudden blasts, or slow decline,
>   Our social comforts drop away.
>   (lines 1–4)

Mines and minds are alike, and Levet's role is to assuage
misery, care, anguish, and want. His "narrow round" (line
25) is not only that of the medical man going from patient to
patient but a narrow circle of being. Yet Johnson locates the
value of Levet's life in this narrow round:

> Then with no throbbing fiery pain,
>   No cold gradations of decay,
> Death broke at once the vital chain,
>   And free'd his soul the nearest way.
>   (lines 33–36)

If the sudden image of the chain, which is the link between
soul and body but also the prisoner's chain, seems to violate
the visual sense of what's gone before, probably that is
intended: the round was still narrower than we'd supposed.
And it only deepens the psychological sense of what's gone
before, confirming the fact that we're condemned, therefore
prisoners chained in the mine. But "vital" chain: that is
Johnson's rhetorical and psychological triumph over circumstance. The chain gives life and sustains it. To be sure,
the image is ambiguous. It takes restraint not to think of any
vital chain as an umbilical cord and any attribution of vital
life to a chain as a longing for the womb. Caverns and mines
confirm the inclination. But it does only a little justice to the
tensile strength of Johnson's empiricism to talk about sub-
limation. Out of his experience, he believed that captivity
was a natural condition and that life could be figured as life
in chains. Different as he was from either Swift or Gay, he
understood the world in the same terms as Swift in the *Tale
of a Tub* or Gay in *The Beggar's Opera*: in the enclosures of

mind and world, we find strength. In the comic arena of the *Tale* and *The Beggar's Opera*, confinement is generative. Swift and Gay think of emergence, they look forward. Johnson has to fight harder against the psychological drag backward to a prenatal state, and he thinks more of release than of rebirth. But all three make the best they can out of the bad deal that fate and the new world seemed to have handed them.

What's more, one could say of Johnson what his old college friend Edwards said of himself, that cheerfulness was always breaking in. Johnson's life, so often punctuated, in Boswell's telling of it by grotesquerie and gaiety, enhances ours as much on that account as for reasons of his tenacity and courage. A fine sentence from Boswell's physical description of Johnson gets to the heart of these things, even though (I think) the emphasis falls a little wrong. As is Boswell's habit and genius, he seizes loose threads of thought from the age and weaves them into the tapestry of Johnson's life: "So morbid was [Johnson's] temperament," Boswell says, "that he never knew the natural joy of a free and vigorous use of his limbs: when he walked, it was like the struggling gait of one in fetters; when he rode, he had no command or direction of his horse, but was carried as if in a balloon" (1398). It is Johnson as a figure from Hogarth, grotesque but full of power when he is on solid earth, and, like Antaeus, bereft of power when he is not.

And—this is why I think Boswell's emphasis is off—we feel the powerfulness of Johnson walking like one in fetters, because Johnson makes us feel it in his life and work, as almost a natural joy, more to be valued than any "free and vigorous" use of the limbs. Limbs are limbs of the body, after all; it is odd to ascribe freedom to them. Perhaps it could only happen after the image of organic harmony, the body and its members, had lost its vitality. Grotesque as it is, the image of Johnson in fetters seems a displaced version of lost harmoniousness in the natural world, another instance of the prison supplanting pastoral freedom. Boswell's cliché about the free and vigorous use of the limbs has a feckless and unconsidered anarchy about it. The joy, if anywhere, is in fact Johnson's, in spite of his morbid temperament, struggling gait and all—or because of them. His struggling gait was the mark, on him, of life's vital chain.

VI

"Like Birds i' th' Cage":
The Poet and the Happy Man

Put your ear to the cage!
You will hear the bustle of little caged poets.
Paolo Buzzi, *"La Gabbia"*[1]

We have watched the artist-figure coming forward, whether as master of revels (*Tom Jones*), or psychic invalid (*Journal of the Plague Year*), or criminal in the eyes of society (*Caleb Williams*). What is yet to happen after the eighteenth century is the forthright appropriation of the artist's consciousness as the central subject of art. For this to happen, not only did the artist have to find ways of separating himself, at least in the imagination, from the world outside the mind, but he also had to find some comfort in isolation —even if only the perverse comfort of despair. The psy-

[1] "The Cage," trans. Dora M. Pettinella in *Arts in Society*, 6 (Spring-Summer, 1969): 113.

chic strategies involved are neatly on display in a literary me-
tempsychosis of the eighteenth century that prepared the
way for (in Paolo Buzzi's witty figure) the modern bustle of
caged poets. In the space vacated by the happy man of
classical tradition, the characteristically happy/unhappy
shut-in of modern tradition—that is to say, the artist or
artist *manqué*—moves in.

Three poems, not of equal merit, show the process at
work. The first is Pope's "Solitude," the poem that he wrote
as a boy and lingered over for many years. The second is
John Norris' "My Estate." Though a step backward in time
to the 1680s, in style to the late Metaphysical mode, and in
competence to something less than the first-rate, still Norris'
poem is in one way a step forward: it displays clearly the
workings of the evolutionary process I will outline. The
third is Blake's "How Sweet I Roam'd," another childhood
effort by another prodigious poet, and the best known of his
Poetical Sketches. Taken together, the three poems display the
most various talents working toward a single, and quite
singular, end.

From its beginnings in Horace's second epode, "Beatus
ille qui procul negotiis . . ."—"happy the man who far
from the cares of business . . ."—and in Virgil's second *Georgic*, the tradition of the happy man took its resonant course
through the poetry of Western Europe.[2] The possibility of
its own subversion was strangely present from the first: the
usurer Alfius is the speaker of Horace's second epode; no
sooner is he done praising rusticity than he returns to
wheeling and dealing. What's more, the tradition grew on a
firm foundation of nostalgia for the golden age ("ut prisca
gens mortalium"), and its tutelary spirit was Silvanus, "tu-

[2]The most comprehensive study of the tradition is Maren-Sofie Røstvig,
The Happy Man: Studies in the Metamorphoses of a Classical Ideal, 2nd ed., 2
vols. (Oslo: Norwegian Universities Press, 1962–1971).

tor finium," as Horace calls him, guardian of boundaries. The rural independence of the happy man, like that of Adam and Eve, was well hedged in. But for all the pristine ambivalence of the form, none would doubt its capacity for sunny hypothesizing. "Wouldn't it be nice if . . .": that is the force of "beatus ille qui procul negotiis." Wouldn't it be nice if there were such a man—or, better still, if oneself were such a man? Nor is it just a hypothesis. Horace gathers a real world of choices within the sylvan boundaries of his hypothesis: "libet iacere modo sub antiqua ilice, / modo in tenaci gramine." It is pleasing sometimes to lie beneath the ancient ilex, sometimes on the matted grass. Now we rejoice in this; now in that. As with irony, the real and the ideal coalesce, but the tradition is not, at bottom, ironical. We may think we have been tricked when we learn who the speaker of the second epode is, but for the time being we have been in Arcady.

If we take a mighty leap, however, and come to the eighteenth century, we discover a new air of sadness and of difficulty surrounding the figure of the happy man, no matter how much compensatory energy the age invested in pursuing (the metaphor of pursuit is symptomatic) happiness. The hypothesis will barely stand up under its own weight. Happy men are often deluded, like Pope's poor Indian, who sees God in clouds and wind, or Swift's fool among knaves. And when Pope seriously tries to breathe life into the tradition, we sense in the turns and twists of his effort an understanding of Johnson's precautionary maxim that much is to be endured and little to be enjoyed. Though Pope claimed to have written "Solitude" at the age of twelve, he did not formally acknowledge it until, at the age of forty-eight, he included it in his collected works (1736). As he revised and revised again this first lisping in verse, it is as if he were trying to lay hands on what was vital to his experience—trying to find out by continuous correction what the boy had had on his mind, or what it was that the poet, looking back, had learned. What in fact he had learned was that the theme of *beatus ille* could survive only as an ironic echo of its classical self.

The earliest text we have, from a letter of 1709, goes like this:[3]

> Happy the man, who free from care,
> The business and the noise of towns,
> Contented breathes his native air,
> > In his own grounds.
>
> Whose herds with milk, whose fields with bread,
> Whose flocks supply him with attire,
> Whose trees in summer yield him shade,
> > In winter fire.
>
> Blest! who can unconcern'dly find
> His years slide silently away,
> In health of body, peace of mind,
> > Quiet by day,
>
> Repose at night; study and ease
> Together mix'd; sweet recreation,
> And innocence, which most does please,
> > With meditation.
>
> Thus let me live, unseen, unknown;
> Thus unlamented let me die;
> Steal from the world, and not a stone
> > Tell where I lie.

In 1717 the poem appeared in print for the first time with three emendations—"unheard" for "unseen" (line 17), "Sound sleep by night" for "Repose at night" (line 13), and "Hours, days and years slide swift away" for "His years

[3] I have used the collation in Pope's *Minor Poems*, ed. Ault and Butt (see Texts Cited), pp. 3–5, for the several texts of "Solitude," and checked it against the originals. I have normalized spelling and accidentals.

slide silently away" (line 10)—and with this rewriting of
stanza one:

> How happy he, who free from care,
> The rage of courts, and noise of towns;
> Contented breathes his native air,
>> In his own grounds.

Hostilities between city and country have deepened. It is no
longer just the innocuous if noisy business of the town being
played off against rural life; it is the rage of courts. Pope
picks up the polemical thread of the tradition and adds it to
his design. At the same time, he has done some damage to
the fabric of his first inspiration. In the earlier version "the
business and the noise of towns" had slipped past easily
enough: an oddly quiet and smooth-flowing line if the point
had been to reproduce the urban hubbub. In fact, the point
was to dampen the noise. Now, in 1717, city and court grow
more clamorous, threatening, emphatically nearby: "the
rage of courts, and noise of towns." The minor emendations
are also in a darker vein. It is worse for a poet to be unheard
than unseen; and years that slide swift away are more con-
ventionally threatening than years that go by silently.

Maybe, then, there's only one thing to do: to shut out the
rage of courts and noise of towns altogether and dedicate
the ode wholly to Silvanus, god of limits and of boundaries.
That is what Pope does in his final revision, the 1736 version
that has found its way into the memories of so many unre-
sisting schoolboys, some of whom it may even have led to
suppose that a rural and tranquil destiny could be their
lot, too:

> Happy the man, whose wish and care
> A few paternal acres bound,
> Content to breathe his native air,
>> In his own ground.

Whose herds with milk, whose fields with bread,
Whose flocks supply him with attire,
Whose trees in summer yield him shade,
        In winter fire.

Blest! who can unconcern'dly find
Hours, days, and years slide soft away,
In health of body, peace of mind,
        Quiet by day,

Sound sleep by night; study and ease
Together mix'd; sweet recreation,
And innocence, which most does please,
        With meditation.

Thus let me live, unseen, unknown;
Thus unlamented let me die;
Steal from the world, and not a stone
        Tell where I lie.

Much has been saved after the darkened version of 1717. The years slide soft rather than swift or even silently away, and the poet lives unseen again, not unheard. There was something faintly silly in that "unheard"—a contradiction in terms like Gray's mute inglorious Miltons. But for anyone tracing Pope's changes, "unheard" turns out to be useful evidence: in 1736, though the poet may be unseen and unknown, even unlamented, we know that this time he's not unheard. What we could hear above all in 1717 were the rage of courts and noise of towns; now we hear the poet, as others will. Nonetheless, what's been saved has been saved at a price. A closer look at that alluring first stanza shows what the price was:

Happy the man, whose wish and care
A few paternal acres bound,
Content to breathe his native air
        In his own ground.

What's been lost is a traditional version of the poet's freedom.

By blocking out the opposition between country and town, Pope also blocks out the norm from which deviation was felt as freedom. This "freedom from" had been indigenous and everywhere in the tradition. Pope could and would have found it in Dryden's and Cowley's translations of Virgil's second *Georgic*—"The swain, who, free from business and debate" (Dryden); and "Free from th'alarms of fear, and storms of strife" (Cowley); or in Cowley's translation of Horace's second epode—"Like the first golden mortals happy he / From bus'ness and the cares of money free!" The revision of stanza one that Pope at last settled on is therefore radical: self becomes absolute, the interplay between the self and external world becomes tricky, language turns in on itself. What was simple and unstudied has grown studiously simple and borders on paradox, as the ambiguities of a Latinate syntax and vocabulary create a little drama of internal and external worlds. "Care" is no longer just anxiety or concern; now it balances between those meanings and the more Latinate meaning of caring for, or, alternatively, those things that are cared for. We are puzzled: are "wish" and "care" parallel terms, each referring to a mental state, or are they poised against each other, the one referring to a mental state, the other to objects of concern in the world outside the mind? And if both refer to mental states, is the care for oneself or for others? In the same way we puzzle over the syntax: what would have been clear from Latin inflections is not so clear in English. Do the few paternal acres set a limit to the happy man's wish and care? It seems so, but because in English we expect subject to come before object, we wonder whether mind measures this world, whether our wish and care set the limits of the land. In either case the drama is of enclosure, perhaps of concentricity: of mind and world alternately encircling each other. In an arrangement like that, even the happy man is not free from care. He's more like Crusoe, imperial ruler of an unpopulated island.

At the same time, Pope's last version of this opening stanza is surely, and by all odds, his best. Taut apposition replaces the looser construction of the earlier versions. The happy man, rather bovine and "contented," becomes a tougher-minded stoic sage: "content to breathe his native air." The ironic drama of self-enclosure creates something humanly stronger than the "freedom from" that the boy-poet inherited from tradition and at first supposed to be the criterion of a happy life. In Thomas Rosenmeyer's words, "Freedom, like simplicity and leisure, is an endowment that the pastoral surrenders at its peril."[4] "Solitude" is not finally in the pastoral mode. Psychodrama has taken over, but the loss is far from total.[5]

Beside Pope, even Pope at the age of twelve, John Norris (1657–1711) was an amateur. But we learn from amateurs, from their slips as well as their successes. "My Estate" (1687) may have been the best known of Norris' poems in his lifetime and after. Perhaps that has something to do with

[4]*The Green Cabinet: Theocritus and the European Pastoral Lyric* (Berkeley and Los Angeles: University of California Press, 1969), p. 129. But, cf. Renato Poggioli, "The Pastoral of the Self," *Daedalus*, 88 (1959): 686–699. Poggioli defines a pastoral of the self that "repudiates all love for any object other than the subject itself" (p. 697), a form of which Rousseau is the "ultimate representative" (p. 687).

[5]On Pope's revisions of the poem, see also Dustin Griffin, "Revisions in Pope's 'Ode on Solitude,'" *Modern Language Quarterly*, 36 (1975): 369–375. In my description of the revisions, I have left out of account a 1726 printing that relies on the 1717 version and a 1727 printing that relies on the version of 1709.

the fact that, for all his Christian orthodoxy, Norris shows in it that he knew more than he could have told about the world that was being born. "My Estate" displays, as clearly as anything could, the coalescence of happy man and captive artist.

The poem begins expansively, in a Metaphysical rhetoric of fits and starts:

> How do I pity that proud wealthy Clown
> That does with Scorn on my low *State* look down!
>   Thy vain Contempt dull *Earth-worm* cease,
>   I won't for Refuge fly to this,
>   That none of Fortune's Blessings can
>   Add any *Value* to the *Man*.
> This *all* the *wise* acknowledge to be *true*;
> But know I am as *rich, more* rich than *you*.
>
> (lines 1–8)

It seems ordinary enough in its own way, unless we're bothered by the direct address of the last line. Is the poet talking to "that proud wealthy Clown"? Or to us as readers, or to a presence we don't know yet? The answer won't be definite until the end, but stanzas two and three clarify matters. The poet is talking, in rather shrill tones, to a landowner and sometime author:

> While you a *Spot* of *Earth* possess with Care
> Below the Notice of the *Geographer*,
>   I by the *Freedom* of my Soul
>   *Possess*, nay more, *enjoy* the *whole*;
>   To th'*Universe* a Claim I lay;
>   Your *Writings* shew perhaps you'll say,
> That's *your* dull Way, my Title runs more *high*,
> 'Tis by the *Charter* of Philosophy.
>
> From that a *firmer* Title I derive
> Than all your *Courts* of *Law* could ever give.
>   A *Title* that more *firm* doth stand

> Than does even *your* very *Land*,
> And yet so generous and free
> That none will e'er *bethink* it me,
> Since my Possessions tend to no Man's *Loss*,
> I all enjoy, yet nothing I ingross.
>
> (lines 9–24)

From the shrillness we can guess that something's amiss.
This is neither the easy Epicureanism of the well-to-do nor
the sufficiency of the small landowner with a few paternal
acres nor the class-conscious social criticism of the disen-
chanted shepherd, nor is it simple Christian affirmation.
Social criticism, which seemed about to overwhelm "Solitude" until Pope took the decisive step of eliminating court
and town, has pushed the poet here into a stance not of
sufficiency but of extravagant self-sufficiency: "To th'*Universe* a Claim I lay . . . . I all enjoy." Can we believe him?

The next stanza, though, looks serene:

> Throughout the Works divine I cast my Eye,
> Admire their *Beauty*, and their *Harmony*.
>   I view the glorious Host above,
>   And him that made them, Praise and Love.
>   The flowry Meads and Fields beneath,
>   Delight me with their odorous Breath.
> Thus is my Joy by you not understood
> Like that of *God*, when he said *all was good*.
>
> (lines 25–32)

The serenity is deceptive. The poet has taken off on a compensatory tour of the skies. Engrossing nothing, he has to
enjoy *every*thing, and that requires the panoramic prospect,
such as God and Newton had, of all things. The last two
lines of the stanza give him away:

> Thus is my Joy by you not understood
> Like that of *God*, when he said *all was good*.

The contentment of the happy man that drained off into social malaise has become the peace—or, here, the joy—of God that passeth all understanding. True, the poet stops short of actually comparing his joy to God's: it is "you" who do not understand it any more than anyone understands God. Still we hear the lurking claim: "Thus is my Joy . . . Like that of *God*, when he said *all was good*." The intervening phrase, "by you not understood," is a smokescreen. This happy man is happy as, at once, author and subject of his own theodicy. God and the happy man, both say all is good. Like Pope in the final version of "Solitude," not to mention the *Essay on Man*, the poet wishes evil into nonbeing. But one stanza is still to go.

Now gravity asserts its pull. Covert ecstasy yields to social criticism that is no longer shrill but offhand, colloquial:

> Nay (what you'd think less likely to be true)
> I can enjoy what's *yours* much more than *you*.
>   Your Meadow's *Beauty* I survey,
>   Which you prize only for its *Hay*.
>   There can I sit beneath a Tree,
>   And write an *Ode* or *Elegy*.
>
> (lines 33–38)

So far, so good, but the turn of the last couplet, still to come, brings us up short:

> What to *you care*, does to *me pleasure* bring,
> You *own* the *Cage*, I in it *sit* and *sing*.
> (lines 39–40)

It is not what we'd bargained for, and quite likely not what Norris had bargained for. Whatever happened to the "wealthy Clown," the "dull *Earth-worm*," of the first stanza, so easy to condescend to? Yet looking back, we can see the

outcome being prepared below the level of conscious inten-
tion. Roles and positions shift rapidly in the poem's first
four lines: the "wealthy Clown," somewhere up there,
"does with Scorn on my low *State* look down!"; then suddenly he's underfoot, a mere worm, food for birds and
therefore perhaps for the speaker should he decide to take
wing ("I won't for Refuge fly to this . . ."). The high-flying
survey of "Works divine" turns out to have been a real
flight; its view of flowers and fields beneath was a true
bird's-eye view, a triumph over earthliness as decisive as
any robin's gobbling up any worm. Only the abrupt and
final metamorphosis of the poet into a caged bird lets us
pick up these (at most) half-intended hints. Still, we are
seeing something important: an intersection of happy man
and captive artist, of sufficiency and self-sufficiency, of ancient and modern. Looking ahead from this poem to Pope's
few paternal acres, we recognize that what Pope discovered
latent in his boyish art was his vocation as a modern poet,
indeed the poet who built his prophetic grotto at Twickenham where he delighted in the fact, as well perhaps as the
symbolism, of refracted light.

Finally, what about the proprietor of the cage: "you"? As
land owner and cage owner, he also owns the songbird-
poet. The grandiose joy of the fourth stanza turns out to
have been wishful thinking. The landless man, hemmed in
by the man of property, discovers that his own disposses-
sion means a loss of control and that one man's loss is
another's gain. It is as if, singing the theme song of the
happy man, the poet had walked into a trap. Having taken
celestial liberties and, now, promising himself enjoyment of
another's goods, he edges nearer to the center of things and
it finishes him. The panoramic view gives way to a restricted
outlook and disorientation: from "Your Meadow's *Beauty* I

survey" to "There can I sit beneath a Tree, / And write an *Ode* or *Elegy*." And as the poet sits *there*, as it were beside himself, the trap is sprung: "You *own* the *Cage*, I in it *sit* and *sing*." A *deus ex machina*, as well as a sinister landlord. The resolution, though it seems final, is in some ways open-ended. Mystery returns as we wonder by what power the landlord imprisons the idle poet so abruptly. A Gothic note touches this metamorphosis of happy man into self-conscious author.

Blake's "How Sweet I Roam'd" follows naturally. T. S. Eliot challenged the proposition that Blake of the *Poetical Sketches* was a child of the Elizabethan poets: "He is very like Collins, he is very eighteenth century."[6] We could answer that Blake is very eighteenth century in that century's neo-Elizabethan mood. In such a mood, Norris would have been a likely model. But one need prove no influence to recognize the point of contact between "My Estate" and "How Sweet I Roam'd":[7]

> How sweet I roam'd from field to field,
>   And tasted all the summer's pride,
> 'Till I the prince of love beheld,
>   Who in the sunny beams did glide!
>
> He shew'd me lilies for my hair,
>   And blushing roses for my brow;
> He led me through his gardens fair,
>   Where all his golden pleasures grow.
>
> With sweet May dews my wings were wet,
>   And Phoebus fir'd my vocal rage;

[6]"William Blake," *Selected Essays*, new edition (New York: Harcourt, Brace, 1950), p. 276.

[7]John Hoyles notices it in *The Waning of the Renaissance, 1640–1740: Studies in the Thought and Poetry of Henry More, John Norris and Isaac Watts* (The Hague: Martinus Nijhoff, 1971), p. 135.

> He caught me in his silken net,
>   And shut me in his golden cage.
>
> He loves to sit and hear me sing,
>   Then, laughing, sports and plays with me;
> Then stretches out my golden wing,
>   And mocks my loss of liberty.

The subject of this teasing poem, it's been said, is marriage
—by analogy to some lines from Quid's song in *An Island
in the Moon*, in which he solicits swains and maidens to come
and be cured of all their pains "in matrimony's golden
cage." But not every golden cage needs to be matrimonial, no matter how many Elizabethan anticipations of the
image one may discover. Granting that wives and golden
cages were proverbially linked, granting that "How Sweet I
Roam'd" has a Petrarchan ring, Norris' poetical cage makes
one think twice. "How Sweet I Roam'd," love song or no,
has as much to do with making poetry as with making love
or getting married.

    After all, we need not suppose at first that the speaker is a
woman. That inference only comes later from the presence
of the prince of love, adorning the speaker with lilies
and roses as though for a wedding. And the weight of
Christian symbolism makes the inference uncertain: we're
all bridal figures in the liturgical drama of Christ and his
church. What's more, the mysterious speaker undergoes
some quick changes—from bee or butterfly to a person
(perhaps a "maiden"), then perhaps to a butterfly again or a
bird ("He caught me in his silken net"), and finally to the
bird of golden wing. Given these changes, why should sexual identity be immutable? Blake's first stanza recalls Spenser's *Muiopotmos*; and the mock-heroic butterfly of that poem
was male:

> The fresh yong flie, in whom the kindly fire
> Of lustfull yougth began to kindle fast,
> Did much disdaine to subiect his desire
> To loathsome sloth, or houres in ease to wast;
> But ioy'd to range abroad in fresh attire,
> Through the wide compas of the ayrie coast . . . .
> (lines 33–38)

Blake's winged creature has the same cheery, almost feck-less fantasies of omnipotence as Spenser's:

> What more felicitie can fall to creature,
> Than to enioy delight with libertie,
> And to be Lord of all the workes of Nature,
> To raine in th'aire from earth to highest skie,
> To feed on flowres, and weeds of glorious feature,
> To take what euer thing doth please the eie?
> (lines 209–214)

Remembering *Muiopotmos*, we might guess not only that the winged creature of Blake's opening lines is male but also, and accurately, that trouble lies ahead. This sense of danger colors the last two lines of stanza one with imprecise fore-boding. It isn't clear why we should fear the prince of love, but we do. Not only do we remember, perhaps, Spenser's butterfly caught in the web of Aragnol; not only do we know that the vagrant pleasures of summer have been inter-rupted; but the prince of love brings both light and dark-ness. On the one hand, he is sunlight; on the other, a sinister, birdlike intruder, his flight like that of a predator casting a quick, disconcerting shadow over "summer's pride."

After this eerie beginning, the wedding scene of stanza two looks oddly like an emasculation; nothing much has changed, gardens are still fair and pleasures golden, but the speaker we may have supposed to be male is not; or not exactly. We have come some way down the road to disor-

ientation, and what follows is even more difficult to fix in
place:

> With sweet May dews my wings were wet,
>   And Phoebus fir'd my vocal rage;
> He caught me in his silken net,
>   And shut me in his golden cage.

For a moment this looks like a flashback. The summer
afternoon of the opening turns into a May morning. But the
metamorphosis of summer into spring, like those of butterfly into person into bird, defies logical construction. We
wonder whether the setting has really changed and wonder
next whether Phoebus is somehow the same as or somehow
different from the prince of love. Both in their way are gods
of the sun, but the metamorphosis turns a vaguely Christian
god into a classical one, turns the language of the King
James version into the diction of eighteenth-century poetry,
and turns the subject of the poem from love to art. The
metamorphosis is, so to speak, of innocence into experience. Phoebus absorbs the quasi-Christian, birdlike god of
the sun, indeed traps him in the cage of his own divinity as
he traps the speaker in the cage of art (like Apollo replacing
Hyperion and usurping the powers of Helios). Therefore
the best answer to the question, Who catches the speaker in
a silken net?, is an odd typology: it is Phoebus as a prince of
love—that is, as the jealous guardian of light construed as
music and art. After the pointed conventionality of "Phoebus fir'd my vocal rage," there's no road back to merely
matrimonial allegory. The poem overflows those boundaries, if in fact they were laid out in the first place:

> He loves to sit and hear me sing,
>   Then, laughing, sports and plays with me;
> Then stretches out my golden wing,
>   And mocks my loss of liberty.

Cruelty overtakes love, and love expires in colloquial abandon: "He loves to sit and hear me sing." It is not just a husband who watches over gilded cage and golden bird. He is too sinister for that. The best commentary I know on this strange poem is that of Alicia Ostriker, who compares the prince of love to Mozart's Queen of the Night. (As the sex of the speaker is indeterminate, so there is something ambivalent about the prince of love and Phoebus, despite their male supremacy.) The "underlying spirit" of it all, she says, "is terror."[8]

Only a writer with the most sensitive nerve endings could have created this brand of terror. For this poem of Blake's childhood, like Pope's "Solitude," both recapitulates and looks ahead. It recapitulates the overthrow of the prince of love by the pagan gods. It recapitulates the theme of the happy man and his overthrow. "How sweet I roam'd from field to field" echoes the tradition of "beatus ille . . ." Reading that first line, we hear overtones of the Augustan poets, even of Pope's second version of "Solitude," "How happy he, who free from care . . .," just as at the end we cannot help hearing echoes of Norris' "You *own* the *Cage*, I in it *sit* and *sing*." At the same time intimations of the future flicker everywhere. If the first line carries the stamp of the past, it also tells of what is coming: because the happy man is done with, like the childhood of the race, recapturing happiness means recapturing childhood or spiraling upward through recovered versions of the self. It also means (we think) getting out of the cage. The burden of the artist turns out not to be (though he may think so) a unique isolation. Rather it is his skill at perceiving what is felt as common isolation. The artist of the caged self, like the ape

[8]*Vision and Verse in William Blake* (Madison and Milwaukee: University of Wisconsin Press, 1965), p. 38.

that drew a picture of the bars around him,[9] turns out to be a realist, portraying no more than what we think we see. Pope and Norris and Blake knew in their bones what was coming.

A sequel to this essay might end with Stephen Dedalus or with midnight cowboys or with the rocket's arc in *Gravity's Rainbow*. It might begin with Coleridge and "This Lime-Tree Bower My Prison":

> Well, they are gone, and here must I remain,
> This lime-tree bower my prison! I have lost
> Beauties and feelings, such as would have been
> Most sweet to my remembrance even when age
> Had dimm'd mine eyes to blindness! They, meanwhile,
> Friends, whom I never more may meet again,
> On springy heath, along the hill-top edge,
> Wander in gladness . . . .

(lines 1–8)

Coleridge's poem reenacts the familiar interchange of stasis and motion, of past and present, though in the idiom of a new age and with the characteristic assertion of a spiral recovery. As his friends, perhaps gone forever, wander (but in gladness) on a springy heath along the edge of a hilltop —a cluster of images that gathers up and transforms the confrontation with limit and limitlessness—the trapped and immobile poet has to make himself a new world, formed from whispered memories of the old. One might carve out yet another definition of the romantic imagination, along these lines, as an interior world of more spacious movement and joy in joys that can't be shared. Coleridge in his bower says that he regains the amplitude of summer, lost feelings and beauties, that the shadow of a bird across the sun makes

---

[9]Vladimir Nabokov tells the story in his afterword to *Lolita* (*The Annotated Lolita*, ed. Alfred Appel, Jr. [New York: McGraw-Hill, 1970], p. 313).

a bond between those who, even at a distance from each other, perceive it:

> My gentle-hearted Charles! when the last rook
> Beat its straight path along the dusky air
> Homewards, I blest it! deeming its black wing
> (Now a dim speck, now vanishing in light)
> Had cross'd the mighty Orb's dilated glory,
> While thou stood'st gazing . . . .
>
> (lines 68–73)

Yet in tracing his way back, he has come on a twilight avatar of Blake's prince of love. The path to what has been lost is the path traveled in losing it. The terror at the beginning of Blake's poem recurs, though muted, as Coleridge comes to the end of his. "This Lime-Tree Bower" and "How Sweet I Roam'd" are reflexive images of each other.

So instead of a sequel, we might settle for one last document from the age when the walls closed in, Cowper's lines (written in September, 1788) on the death of Mrs. Throckmorton's bullfinch:

> Just then, by adverse fate impress'd,
> A dream disturb'd poor Bully's rest;
>   In sleep he seem'd to view
> A rat, fast-clinging to the cage,
> And, screaming at the sad presage,
>   Awoke and found it true.
>
> For, aided both by ear and scent,
> Right to his mark the monster went—
>   Ah, Muse! forbear to speak
> Minute the horrors that ensued;
> His teeth were strong, the cage was wood—
>   He left poor Bully's beak.
>
> He left it—but he should have ta'en.
> That beak, whence issued many a strain
>   Of such mellifluous tone,

Might have repaid him well, I wote,
For silencing so sweet a throat,
    Fast set within his own.

Maria weeps—The Muses mourn—
So, when by Bacchanalians torn,
    On Thracian Hebrus' side

"L'Entrée de la prison ou la mise en cage" by
Hubert Robert.

The tree-enchanter Orpheus fell;
His head alone remain'd to tell
The cruel death he died.
(lines 43–66)

The literature of the age has more than its share of captive birds—Sophia's pet, released by Blifil and carried away by a "nasty Hawk"; or Yorick's heraldic starling, whose only words are "I can't get out"; but none more tragical-comical

"La Sortie de la prison ou les oiseaux en liberté" by Hubert Robert. (Reproduced from Pierre de Nolhac, *Hubert Robert, 1733–1808*, Paris: Goupil, 1910.)

and symptomatic than Mrs. Throckmorton's bullfinch.[10]
Bully's fate is a domestic he-tragedy, a parody of Adam's
dream, but also a dream of release. Though the moral of the
story seems to be that birds had better live in wire cages, the
melancholic Cowper takes a sad subterranean delight in
Mrs. Throckmorton's improvidence. A wire cage would
only have postponed the issue. To be broken in upon by
death is how Cowper dreams release will come. To Yorick
and to Blifil (not an impossible pairing, once one has made
the large allowances necessary for Blifil's wickedness and
hypocrisy) and to how many others since them, the dream
has been of breaking out. The fatal release of Sophia's bird
and the confinement of Yorick's starling, mechanically re-
peating "I can't get out, I can't get out," seem like pre-
visionary comments on our own fantastical lives. Between
the dreams of breaking out and of being broken in upon we
still restlessly swing.

[10]See Fielding, *Tom Jones*, intro. Battestin, ed. Bowers (see Texts Cited),
p. 160; and Sterne, *A Sentimental Journey through France and Italy*, ed. Gardner
D. Stout, Jr. (Berkeley and Los Angeles: University of California Press,
1967) p. 197f. Lorenz Eitner discusses the iconography of caged birds in a
forthcoming article.

Texts Cited

PROSE

Beckford, William. *Vathek*, ed., with an Introduction, by Roger Lonsdale (Oxford English Novels). London: Oxford University Press, 1970.

Boswell, James. *Life of Johnson* (Oxford Standard Authors, new ed.). London: Geoffrey Cumberlege, Oxford University Press, 1953.

Defoe, Daniel. *The Fortunes and Misfortunes of the Famous Moll Flanders*, ed., with an Introduction, by G. A. Starr (Oxford English Novels). London: Oxford University Press, 1971.

_____. *A Journal of the Plague Year*, ed., with an Introduction, by Louis Landa (Oxford English Novels). London: Oxford University Press, 1969.

_____. *The Life and Strange Surprizing Adventures of Robinson Crusoe, of York, Mariner*, ed., with an Introduction, by J. Donald Crowley (Oxford English Novels). London: Oxford University Press, 1972.

Fielding, Henry. *The History of Tom Jones, A Foundling*, with an Introduction and Commentary by Martin C. Battestin, the Text Edited by Fredson Bowers (Wesleyan Edition of the Works of Henry Fielding), 2 vols. Middletown, Conn.: Wesleyan University Press, 1975.

Gay, John. *The Beggar's Opera*, with Commentaries by Louis Kronenberger and Max Goberman. Larchmont, N.Y.: Argonaut Books, 1961.

Godwin, William. *Caleb Williams*, ed., with an Introduction, by David McCracken (Oxford English Novels). London: Oxford University Press, 1970.

Johnson, Samuel. *The History of Rasselas, Prince of Abissinia*, ed., with an Introduction, by Geoffrey Tillotson and Brian Jenkins (Oxford English Novels). London: Oxford University Press, 1971.

————. "Milton," in *Lives of the English Poets*, ed. George Birkbeck Hill; *Vol. I: Cowley-Dryden*. Oxford: Clarendon Press, 1905.

————. *The Rambler*, ed. W. J. Bate and Albrecht B. Strauss, Vols. III and IV of *The Yale Edition of the Works of Samuel Johnson*. New Haven: Yale University Press, 1969.

Smollett, Tobias. *The Adventures of Roderick Random* (Shakespeare Head Edition of Smollett's Novels), 2 vols. Oxford: Basil Blackwell, 1925–1926.

Sterne, Laurence. *The Life and Opinions of Tristram Shandy, Gentleman*, ed. James Aiken Work. New York: Odyssey Press, 1940.

Swift, Jonathan. *Gulliver's Travels*, ed. Herbert Davis, with an Introduction by Harold Williams, Vol. XI of *The Prose Writings of Jonathan Swift*. Oxford: Basil Blackwell, 1965.

————. *A Tale of a Tub, To which is added The Battle of the Books and the Mechanical Operation of the Spirit*, ed., with an Introduction and Notes Historical and Explanatory, by A. C. Guthkelch and D. Nichol Smith, 2nd ed. Oxford: Clarendon Press, 1958.

POETRY

Addison, Joseph. "Ode: The Spacious Firmament on High," in *Eighteenth-Century English Literature*, ed. Geoffrey Tillotson, Paul Fussell, Jr., and Marshall Waingrow, with the assistance of Brewster Rogerson. New York: Harcourt, Brace & World, 1969, p. 823.

Blake, William. "Song: How Sweet I Roam'd," in *Eighteenth-Century English Literature*, ed. Tillotson, Fussell, and Waingrow, p. 1492.

Coleridge, Samuel Taylor. "This Lime-Tree Bower My Prison" and "The Rime of the Ancient Mariner," in *English Romantic Writers*, ed. David Perkins. New York: Harcourt, Brace & World, 1967, pp. 403–404, 404–413.

Cowper, William. "On the Death of Mrs. Throckmorton's Bulfinch," in *Cowper: Selected Poems and Letters*, ed. A. Norman Jeffares (New Oxford English Series). London: Oxford University Press, 1963, pp. 79–81.

Denham, John. *Coopers Hill*, in *Expans'd Hieroglyphicks: A Critical Edition of Sir John Denham's Coopers Hill*, by Brendan O Hehir. Berkeley and Los Angeles: University of California Press, 1969, pp. 77–162.

Dyer, John. *Grongar Hill*, in *Eighteenth-Century English Literature*, ed. Tillotson, Fussell, and Waingrow, pp. 807–810 (Pindaric and octosyllabic versions).

Johnson, Samuel. *The Vanity of Human Wishes* and "On the Death of Dr. Robert Levet," in *The Yale Edition of the Works of Samuel Johnson; Vol. VI: Poems*, ed. E. L. McAdam, Jr., with George Milne. New Haven: Yale University Press, 1964, pp. 90–109, 313–315.

Keats, John. "To Autumn," in *English Romantic Writers*, ed. Perkins, p. 1204.

Milton, John. *Paradise Lost* and *Lycidas*, in *Complete Poems and Major Prose*, ed. Merritt Y. Hughes. New York: Odyssey Press, 1957, pp. 173–469, 116–125.

Norris, John. "My Estate," in *A Collection of Miscellanies: Consisting of Poems, Essays, Discourses & Letters, Occasionally Written*, 5th ed. London, 1710, pp. 58–59.

Pope, Alexander. *Eloisa to Abelard*, "Ode on Solitude," and "Mary Gulliver to Captain Lemuel Gulliver," in *The Twickenham Edition of the Poems of Alexander Pope; Vol. II: The Rape of the Lock and Other Poems*, ed. Geoffrey Tillotson, and *Vol. VI: Minor Poems*, ed. Norman Ault and John Butt. London: Methuen & Co.; Vol. II, 3rd ed., 1962, pp. 293–349; Vol. VI, 1954, pp. 3–5, 276–279.

Rochester, John Wilmot, Earl of. "A Satyr Against Reason and Mankind," in *The Complete Poems of John Wilmot, Earl of Rochester*, ed. David M. Vieth. New Haven: Yale University Press, 1968, pp. 94–101.

Spenser, Edmund. *Muiopotmos: or The Fate of the Butterflie*, in *The Works of Edmund Spenser: A Variorum Edition*, ed. Edwin Greenlaw, Charles Grosvenor Osgood, Frederick Morgan Padelford, and Ray Heffner; *The Minor Poems, Vol. II*, ed. Charles Grosvenor Osgood, Henry Gibbons Lotspeich, and Dorothy E. Mason. Baltimore: Johns Hopkins Press, 1947, pp. 155–173.

Swift, Jonathan. "A Description of the Morning" and "A Description of a City Shower," in *The Poems of Jonathan Swift*, ed. Harold Williams, Vol. I, 2nd ed. Oxford: Clarendon Press, 1958, pp. 123–125, 136–139.

Wordsworth, William. *The Prelude: or Growth of a Poet's Mind*, in *English Romantic Writers*, ed. Perkins, pp. 212–263.

Index

Addison, Joseph, 15, 60, 61
Adventurer, The (Zweig), 2n
Altamira, caves of, ix
America: Johnson on, 147–149, 153; escape to, 149, 151f
"Ancient Mariner, The" (Coleridge), 144f
Aristotle, 14, 35
Arnold, Matthew, 26
Artists, 61, 171f, 187; as observers, 20f, 57, 69f, 77, 79; captive, 23, 179, 182; individual characters as, 75–81, 120f, 134; escape, 78, 137, 143
Augustan writers, 24, 187

Balloon flight, 21, 103, 107, 157
Barker, Robert, 102f, 107, 157
Baudelaire, Charles, 9
"Beatus ille", *See* Happy man
Beckett, Samuel, 48, 167
Beckford, William, *Vathek*, 18, 21, 103, 119, 135–142
Beggar's Opera, The (Gay), 20, 62f, 87–89, 94–101, 168f
Benardete, José, 114f
Bentham, Jeremy: *Panopticon*, 20f, 21n, 75, 78f
Berkeley, George, x, 10–17 *passim*, 88, 148
Bernardin de Saint Pierre, Jacques Henri, 60

Binny, John, 4n
Birds, images of, 134, 157, 160, 182, 191f; in Blake, 184–187
Bird's-eye views, 11, 165, 182
Blake, William, 23–25, 172, 183–189
Boswell, James, 147, 148, 150f, 169f
Boyd, D. V., 167n
Brombert, Victor, 2f, 167n
Brown, Homer O., 58
Bunyan, John, 30
Buzzi, Paolo, 171
Byrd, Max, 19
Byron, George Gordon, Lord, 86

Cages: images of birds in, 134, 182, 187, 192; as metaphors for art, 172, 182–188
Caleb Williams (Godwin), 21, 103, 119, 127–134, 144, 171
Camus, Albert, 67
Captives and captivity: fictions of, 61–67; in Defoe, 78; in Swift, 89; Johnson on, 147, 168, 179, 182. *See also* Prisons
Carceri (Piranesi), 9f, 15
Castle of Otranto, The (Walpole), 150
Circles, 9, 60; traced by journeys, 104, 117, 125f, 127, 144, 168
Cities, 43, 79f; confinement in, 19, 20, 67–80 *passim*; vs. country, 81, 97, 175

"City Shower" (Swift), 62, 67, 69–71, 79

Clarissa (Richardson), 18, 61, 66

Coleridge, Samuel Taylor, 22, 104, 144f, 188f

Common Sky, A (Nuttall), 11n

Confinement, x, 2–8 *passim*, 15, 19–21, 61, 103; in Swift, 62; in Defoe, 71f; in Pope, 81, 86; in Johnson, 162. *See also* Prisons

Conrad, Joseph, 26

Coopers Hill (Denham), x, 18, 21, 103, 108–117

Cowley, Abraham, 151–153, 155, 160, 177

Cowper, William, 189–192

Criminal Prisons of London and Scenes of Prison Life, The (Mayhew and Binny), 4n

Crusoe. *See* Robinson Crusoe

"Day of Judgement, The" (Swift), 68n

Death: as release, 19, 96, 104; Tristram's flight from, 21, 103, 119–125; figures of, 72, 120, 133; dance of, 72f, 81, 83, 120f, 133, 137; in *A Journal of the Plague Year*, 72f; in *Eloisa to Abelard*, 81–94 *passim*; in *Caleb Williams*, 128, 130, 133; in *Rasselas*, 155, 160

Defoe, Daniel, 9, 67, 142; *Moll Flanders*, 19, 61, 63–67, 95; *A Journal of the Plague Year*, 20, 62, 71–79, 81, 90, 171; *Serious Reflections . . .* , 45n. See also *Robinson Crusoe*

Denham, John, 18, 21, 108–117, 136

De Quincey, Thomas, 9

"Description of the Morning" (Swift), 62, 67–70, 79

Dictionary (Johnson), 153, 166n

"Digression on Madness" (Swift), 92f

"Dr. Johnson's Refutation of Bishop Berkeley" (Hallett), 148n

Don Juan (Byron), 86

Donne, John, 26

Dryden, John, 71, 177

Durfey, Tom, 97–99

Dyer, John, 62, 80f, 162f

Eliot, T. S., 183

Ellison, Ralph, 43

Eloisa to Abelard (Pope), 19, 62, 81–87, 90, 94, 119

Émile (Rousseau), 35

Empson, William, 99

Escape: metaphors of, 2; artists, 78, 137, 143; fantasies of, 135, 147, 149, 151, 160. *See also* Flight

Essay on Man (Pope), 181

Field, Erastus Salisbury, 26

Fielding, Henry, 66f, 92; *Tom Jones*, 19, 61, 64, 66, 80, 94–96, 171, 191f

Flight: theme of, x, 2, 21f, 101, 103f; in Pascal, 12; in Rochester, 16f; balloon, 21, 103, 107, 157; of Tristram, 21, 119–127; Johnson and, 22, 149–162, 166f; in Defoe, 74; in Swift's *Tale*, 104–108; in Denham, 110–112; of Milton's Satan, 117–119; in Godwin, 119, 127–134; in Beckford, 135–142; in Wordsworth, 142–145; in Coleridge, 144–145; in Keats, 146; in Norris, 182

Fonthill Abbey, 135

Ford, Ford Madox, 56f

Foucault, Michel, ix, 21n

Freud, Sigmund, 3

From the Closed World to the Infinite Universe (Koyré), 8n

Gay, John: *The Beggar's Opera*, 20, 62f, 87–89, 94–101, 168f

Genet, Jean, 1f

Georgics (Virgil), 172, 177

Gnosticism, 100, 106

Godwin, William: *Caleb Williams*, 21, 103, 119, 127–134, 144, 171

Good Soldier, The (Ford), 56f

Gothicism, 1, 10, 17, 37, 65, 103,

127, 142; and Johnson, 150, 152, 161; and Norris, 183
Gravity's Rainbow (Pynchon), 188
Gray, Thomas, 176
Grongar Hill (Dyer), 62, 80f, 162f
Gulliver's Travels (Swift), 19, 27, 29f, 41–59 *passim*, 67, 152

Hagstrum, Jean, 141n
Hallett, H. F., 148n
Happy man, tradition of, 172–187 *passim*
Hassan, Ihab, 29
Heart of Darkness (Conrad), 26
Heisenberg, Werner, 3
Heller, Joseph, 2
Hogarth, William, 169
Horace, 86, 172f, 177
"How Sweet I Roam'd" (Blake), 23f, 172, 183–189
Hugo, Victor, 9
"Hunger Artist, The" (Kafka), 133f
Huxley, Aldous, 20

Icarus, 16, 22, 160
Imprisonment. *See* confinement; Prisons
Infinite universe, 7–15 *passim*, 154
Infinity, 16–18, 60, 135, 167; Kant on, 87f, 114; Benardete on, 114f
Irony, x, 19, 88, 173; in Swift, 87, 91; in Gay, 87, 97; in Johnson, 162
Island in the Moon, An (Blake), 184
Islands, 19, 26, 29f, 37, 49, 55f, 58; in Rousseau, 27f; Pascal's image of, 28f; in *Robinson Crusoe*, 30–45, 57, 178; in *Gulliver's Travels*, 48, 49; in *Tristram Shandy*, 55f; in Cowley, 151f

James, Henry, 20, 76
Johnson, Samuel, 3, 11f, 22f, 146, 173; *Rasselas*, 22, 153–162, 164; *The Vanity of Human Wishes*, x, 22, 162–167; and Boswell, 147–151, 169f; and the "American savage", 147–149; on Milton,

149–151; on Cowley, 151–153; *Rambler*, 151, 156, 167n; *Dictionary*, 153, 166n; "On the Death of Dr. Robert Levet", 167f
Journal of the Plague Year, A (Defoe), 20, 62, 71–79, 81, 90, 171
Joyce, James, 160

Kafka, Franz, 133f
Kant, Immanuel, 87f, 114
Keats, John, 7, 22, 104, 146
Kepler, Johannes, 10, 17
Koyré, Alexandre, 8n

Language: Gulliver and, 45–54; in *Tristram Shandy*, 54–56; Johnson on, 147–151; in Pope, 177
Lawrence, D. H., 26f
Lefebvre, Henri, 34
Life of Samuel Johnson (Boswell), 147
Locke, John, 7, 15, 40, 76, 153, 156
London, 62, 83, 89, 102, 112
London Labour and the London Poor (Mayhew), 4n
Lucretius, 16
Ludwig Wittgenstein: A Memoir (Malcolm), 147n
Lycidas (Milton), 149–151

"Madhouse, the Whorehouse and the Convent, The" (Byrd), 19
Madness and Civilization (Foucault), ix
Malcolm, Norman, 147n
Malebranche, Nicolas de, 166
Mallarmé, Stephane, 60
Martial, 100
"Mary Gulliver to Captain Lemuel Gulliver" (Pope), 51
Mayhew, Henry, 4n
Melville, Herman, 39
Milton, John, 106, 152, 160; *Paradise Lost*, 21, 103f, 117–119; *Lycidas*, 149–151; Johnson on, 149–151
Miracle of the Rose (Genet), 1f
Modern Heroism (Sale), ix
Modest Proposal, A (Swift), 67

Moll Flanders (Defoe), 19, 61, 63–67, 95
Montgolfier. *See* Balloon flight
Muiopotmos (Spenser), 184f
"My Estate" (Norris), 23, 172, 178–183, 187

Newton, Sir Isaac, 180
Nominalism, 49
Norris, John, 23, 172, 178–184, 187f
Nuttall, A. D., 11n

"Ode on Solitude" (Pope), 23, 172–178, 180f, 187
O Hehir, Brendan, 108f, 111
"On the Death of Dr. Robert Levet" (Johnson), 167f
Ostriker, Alicia, 187
Ovid, 86

Panopticon; or, the Inspection House (Bentham), 20f, 78f
Panorama, invention of, 21, 102f, 107, 114f
Panoramic views: in poetry, 16f, 162, 164, 180, 182
Paradise: regained, 62, 153; in Milton, 104, 117f, 151; in *Tristram Shandy*, 119f, 125; in *Vathek*, 119, 141f
Paradise Lost (Milton), 21, 103f, 117–119
Pascal, Blaise, x, 4; on "petit cachot", 7, 10, 12–14, 17; on islands, 17, 27–32 *passim*; and Crusoe, 32, 36f, 40
Pastoral: tradition of, 67, 89, 103, 150, 170, 178; in Dyer, 62; in Pope, 62, 81, 178; in Gay, 62, 89, 94–100 *passim*; in Swift, 89, 94; in Godwin, 132; Johnson on, 149–152
Piranesi, Giambattista, x, 9f, 14f, 106, 135, 139
Plato, 55, 60
Pliny, 35
Poetical Sketches (Blake), 172, 183

Pope, Alexander, x, 42f, 89, 182, 188; *Eloisa to Abelard*, 19, 62, 81–87, 90, 94, 119; *The Rape of the Lock*, 34f; "Mary Gulliver to Captain Lemuel Gulliver", 51; "Ode on Solitude", 23, 172–178, 180f, 187; *Essay on Man*, 181
Poulet, Georges, 8f, 60, 87f
Prelude, The (Wordsworth), 142–144
Primitivism, myth of, 147–149
Prisons: as image, 1–9 *passim*, 26, 103, 170; real, 4; happy, 19f, 61–66, 87, 91; journal of life in, 24f; in Pascal, 28f; in Swift, 62, 67, 69, 95; in Defoe, 62, 78; in Gay, 62f, 95–97; Johnson and, 156, 170
Prisoner's Opera, The (Ward), xi
Prospect poetry, 21, 103, 108–119 *passim*
Prospects: in *The Vanity of Human Wishes*, 22, 162, 166; in *Coopers Hill*, 110–114; in *Tristram Shandy*, 125; in *Vathek*, 136; in *Rasselas*, 153–155, 164; in *Grongar Hill*, 164; in "My Estate", 180
Pynchon, Thomas, 188

Quest, motif of, 21f, 103f, 127, 130, 134, 140

Rabelais, François, 55
Rambler (Johnson), 151, 156, 167n
Rape of the Lock, The (Pope), 34f
Rasselas (Johnson), 22, 153–162, 164
Realism: modes of, 29, 188; in *Robinson Crusoe*, 32, 37, 56; in *Tristram Shandy*, 56; in *The Beggar's Opera*, 95, 99
Reynolds, Sir Joshua, 103
Richardson, Samuel, 18, 61, 66
Robinson Crusoe, 19, 27–45, 48f, 125, 144, 148, 154, 178; compared to Gulliver and Toby, 53–59 *passim*, 152
Robinson Crusoe (Defoe), x, 30–45, 55, 58f, 143

Rochester, John Wilmot, Earl of, x, 16f
Roderick Random (Smollett), 61, 63–65, 67, 95
Romanticism, x, 104, 188
Rosenmeyer, Thomas, 178
Rousseau, Henri, 26
Rousseau, Jean-Jacques, 27f, 30, 31, 35, 37, 40

Sale, Roger, ix
Sartre, Jean-Paul, 131
Satire, 46, 53, 109
"Satyr Against Reason and Mankind, A" (Rochester), 16f
Schiele, Egon, 24f
Serious Reflections . . . (Defoe), 45n
Sexuality, 1, 17, 19; and island life, 29, 55; in *Robinson Crusoe*, 19, 33, 49; in *Gulliver's Travels*, 19, 48f; in *Tristram Shandy*, 19, 49, 53; in *Eloisa to Abelard*, 83; in *Caleb Williams*, 130
Shakespeare, William, 7
Silence, 4, 19, 29, 84, 96, 119, 146; in Defoe, 34, 38–44 *passim*, 75; in Swift, 47f, 51, 67, 69
Silvanus, 172, 175
Smollett, Tobias George, 61, 63–65, 67, 95
Socrates, 106, 117
Something Happened (Heller), 2
Spenser, Edmund, 30, 184f
Spirals, 104, 144–146
Starobinski, Jean, 21
Sterne, Laurence, 19, 30, 54, 55, 58, 121, 123. See also *Tristram Shandy*
Surveiller et punir: Naissance de la prison (Foucault), 21n
Swift, Jonathan, x, 3, 18, 58, 75, 173; *Gulliver's Travels*, 19, 27, 29f, 41–59 *passim*, 67, 152; *Tale of a Tub*, 20, 62f, 87–96, 100, 104–108, 127, 168f; "Description of the Morning", 62, 67–69, 70, 79; "City Shower", 67, 69–71, 79; *A Modest Proposal*, 67; "The Day of Judgement", 68n; "Digression on Madness", 92f

Tale of a Tub (Swift), 20, 62f, 87–96, 100, 104–108, 127, 168f
"This Lime-Tree Bower My Prison" (Coleridge), 188f
Thrale, Hester, 22
Three Dialogues between Hylas and Philonous (Berkeley), 10f
"To Autumn" (Keats), 146
Tom Jones (Fielding), 19, 61, 64, 66, 80, 94–96, 171, 191f
Traugott, John, 55n
Tristram Shandy (Sterne), x, 45, 119–127, 156; Uncle Toby in, 19, 27, 29f, 41f, 45, 53–59, 119, 126, 152; Tristram in, 21, 54f, 58, 103, 119–127, 154
Tuveson, Ernest, 14
Twickenham, Pope's grotto at, 42, 182

"Upon his Majesties repairing of Pauls" (Waller), 111f

Vanity of Human Wishes, The (Johnson), x, 22, 162–167
Vathek (Beckford), 18, 21, 103, 119, 135–142
Vigny, Alfred de, 9
Virgil, 172, 177

Waller, Edmund, 111f
Ward, Ned, xi
Wittgenstein, Ludwig, 147
Wordsworth, William, 22, 104, 142–145

Zweig, Paul, 2n